THE TENSION OF THE LYRE

To Florence and Maynard
with the author's affection
and best wishes,

Hallett

SHAKE-SPEARES

SONNETS.

Neuer before Imprinted.

pretium — ſ̄ N. L. Sᵗ.

Gloria virtutis merces.

George Steevens.

AT LONDON
By *G. Eld* for *T. T.* and are
to be ſolde by *Iohn Wright,* dwelling
at Chriſt Church gate.
1609.

*This title page and the other reproductions
in this volume are taken from the 1609 Quarto
in the Huntington Library*

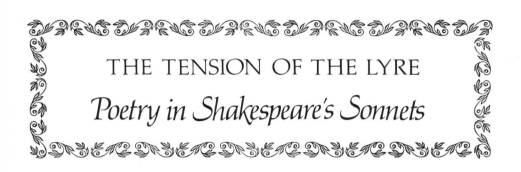

THE TENSION OF THE LYRE
Poetry in Shakespeare's Sonnets

by HALLETT SMITH

HUNTINGTON LIBRARY
SAN MARINO, CALIFORNIA
1981

Library of Congress Cataloging in Publication Data

Smith, Hallett Darius, 1907–
    The Tension of the Lyre

    Bibliography: p. 163
    Includes index.
    1. Shakespeare, William, 1564–1616. Sonnets.
2. Sonnets, English—History and criticism.
 I. Title.
PR2848.S6   821's   80–39610
ISBN 0–87328–114–4

TABLE OF CONTENTS

I speak below the

The tension of the lyre

Wallace Stevens, "St. John and the Backache."

PREFACE

This book is based upon the conviction that a useful discussion of Shakespeare's sonnets will not make them more complicated than they seem to be, but less so. I do not claim that they are simple; the poems contain complexities of rhetoric, of diction, and of sound. But even these complexities, in my opinion, have their limits, and I have tried to stay within them.

I quote the sonnets frequently, because I wish the reader to apply my critical remarks, and others which I cite, to the sonnets themselves as readily as possible. I also consciously repeat quotations as the context varies. An index of sonnets and parts of sonnets quoted will enable anyone to collect all I have to say about a passage. The text I use is that of *The Riverside Shakespeare,* though I have at times felt free to alter the punctuation.

The six chapters are not uniformly designed, yet they are the product of a single impulse—to make the sonnets more accessible to various kinds of readers. Besides Shakespeare scholars and critics, whose good opinion I hope for, I have in mind three others. The first is a lady whose name I have forgotten. She served on a jury with me, and while the court was in recess, as it often was, we talked about common interests and she said she had not found anything very helpful on the subject of Shakespeare's sonnets. I have in mind also a professor of engineering who used to meet me on the campus and recite another Shakespeare sonnet he had just memorized. (He may think my quotations are unnecessary.) And I have in mind a wise and genial editor who has nudged me gently, ever since the publication of my *Shakespeare's Romances* (1972), to write something on the sonnets. Jane Evans and Holly Bridges helped transform this from foul papers to printed book.

I am indebted to several good friends—James Thorpe, Elizabeth Pomeroy, Betty Leigh Merrell, Paul M. Zall, Jenijoy LaBelle, and Mary Ellis Arnett—for help of many kinds. I am conscious of a very great obligation to the anonymous publisher's reader for his acute and thorough commentary on the manuscript. I owe a great deal to the Variorum edition of the sonnets by Hyder E. Rollins and to the recent analytical commentary by Stephen Booth. I have profited from his edition, but I have, I trust, shaken myself loose from many of its tentacles. My main objection to his commentary is that he accepts completely William Empson's dictum that *all* suggested glosses for a passage are right. (See his edition, p. xiii.) I rather hold, with Empson's master, I. A. Richards, that there are such things as irrelevant associations, and that these can impede or impair the proper understanding and appreciation of a poem.

I often refer to "readers" of the sonnets, and I devote a final chapter to some of them. I might well have said "listeners," for these poems must be heard. They are not sound and fury, signifying nothing, but sound and sense, signifying everything. "What's in the brain that ink may character?" asks the first line of Sonnet 108. There is much in the sonnets to answer that question.

W. H. Auden opened his introduction to the Signet Classic edition of the sonnets by declaring that more nonsense has been written about them than about any other literary work in the world. This book may also be nonsense. If so, I hope it is what Alfred North Whitehead would call "the right *kind* of nonsense."

THE TENSION OF THE LYRE

Abbreviations

ELH	English Literary History
JEGP	Journal of English and Germanic Philology
MLQ	Modern Language Quarterly
MLR	Modern Language Review
MP	Modern Philology
N&Q	Notes and Queries
PMLA	Publications of the Modern Language Association of America
RES	Review of English Studies
SEL	Studies in English Literature
SQ	Shakespeare Quarterly
TLS	The Times (London) Literary Supplement
TSLL	Texas Studies in Language and Literature
UTQ	University of Toronto Quarterly

CHAPTER ONE

The Voices and the Audience in Shakespeare's Sonnets

T. S. Eliot maintained that there are three voices of poetry. "The first voice," he said, "is the voice of the poet talking to himself—or to nobody. The second is the voice of the poet addressing an audience, whether large or small. The third is the voice of the poet when he attempts to create a dramatic character speaking in verse."[1] With the third voice we have nothing to do in considering the sonnets, though of course it is primary in any study of the plays. With the first two voices we shall be much concerned. The first voice requires some explanation.

Poems in which the poet seems to be talking to himself, or to nobody, are commonly reflective poems, poems of meditation, if we use that term in its most general sense. Shakespeare shows us one such poem in the process of composition, at the end of *Richard II.* There the deposed king, in prison, is trying to compare his prison to the world. There is no audience; he is speaking to himself, or to nobody. He has trouble making the comparison, until he realizes that, just as the world is crowded with people, so his prison is inhabited by thoughts.

> And these same thoughts people this little world,
> In humors like the people of this world:
> For no thought is contented.
>
> (V, v, 9–11)[2]

His poem is full of contradictions, of opposites—king and beggar, music and discord, the man who wastes time and the man who is

---

[1] "The Three Voices of Poetry" (1953), in *On Poetry and Poets* (1957), p. 96.
[2] All Shakespeare quotations are from *The Riverside Shakespeare*, ed. G. Blakemore Evans *et. al.* (1974).

wasted by time. The music he hears drives him mad, though it is supposed to cure madness:

> This music mads me, let it sound no more,
> For though it have holp mad men to their wits,
> In me it seems it will make wise men mad.
> Yet blessing on his heart that gives it me!
> For 'tis a sign of love; and love to Richard
> Is a strange brooch in this all-hating world.

(V, v, 61–66)

Shakespeare's Sonnet 94, a famous and difficult one, may be a meditation directed to himself or to nobody:

> They that have pow'r to hurt, and will do none,
> That do not do the thing they most do show,
> Who moving others, are themselves as stone,
> Unmoved, cold, and to temptation slow,
> They rightly do inherit heaven's graces,
> And husband nature's riches from expense;
> They are the lords and owners of their faces,
> Others but stewards of their excellence.
> The summer's flow'r is to the summer sweet,
> Though to itself it only live and die,
> But if that flow'r with base infection meet,
> The basest weed outbraves his dignity:
>> For sweetest things turn sourest by their deeds;
>> Lilies that fester smell far worse than weeds.

There may be several reminiscences of New Testament passages here, but one that is certain is Matt. 6:28–29, "And why take ye thought for raiment? Consider the lilies of the field, how they grow; they toil not, neither do they spin: And yet I say unto you, That even Solomon in all his glory was not arrayed like one of these." There may also be a recollection of a passage in John Gerard's preface to his *Herball* (1597) which speaks of "one King Salomon, excelling all the rest for wisdome, of greater royalty than they all (though the Lillies of the field outbraued him.)"

Older interpretations of the sonnet, such as Empson's and Ransom's,[3] are based on the notion that the sonnet is addressed to the

---

[3] See my *Elizabethan Poetry* (1952), p. 189.

2

Fair Friend, though there is no internal evidence that this is so. I believe Melchiori is right when he says, "Sonnet 94, like sonnets 121, 129, 146, is a soliloquy in so far as it has to *get away* from the *private* context of the surrounding poems, and to debate, before the sessions of the poet's silent thought, matters of general concern."[4]

Of course the soliloquy and its shorter form, the aside, belong to a convention naturally and inevitably used by Elizabethan playwrights. The aside most often serves the purpose of revealing to the audience, though not to the other characters on the stage, someone's true feelings. Cordelia's comments after her sisters' flattering speeches are an example: "What shall Cordelia speak? Love, and be silent" and "Then poor Cordelia! / And yet not so, since I am sure my love's / More ponderous than my tongue" (*King Lear* I, i, 62–63, 76–78). But the aside may reveal viciousness as well as virtue, as in Richard Duke of Gloucester's asides when his nephew, young Prince Edward, expresses pious thoughts: "So wise so young, they say do never live long" (*Richard III,* III, i, 79).

The soliloquy is sometimes used for the same purpose as the aside: to inform the audience that the character's actions, and perhaps even speech, are not to be taken at face value. The soliloquy serves, then, as an artificial means of conveying from the dramatist to the audience a message which the playwright cannot convey directly. The character delivers the message, even though at times it is inconsistent with his character or at least with those traits that have so far been established on the stage. A classical case is Prince Hal's soliloquy at the end of the first tavern scene in *1 Henry IV:*

> I know you all, and will a while uphold
> The unyok'd humor of your idleness,
> Yet herein will I imitate the sun,
> Who doth permit the base contagious clouds
> To smother up his beauty from the world,
> That when he please again to be himself,
> Being wanted, he may be more wond'red at
> By breaking through the foul and ugly mists
> Of vapors that did seem to strangle him.
>
> (I, ii, 195–203)

[4]Georgio Melchiori, *Shakespeare's Dramatic Meditations: An Experiment in Criticism* (1976), p. 68. J. W. Lever reached a similar conclusion: *The Elizabethan Love Sonnet* (1956), pp. 216–17.

3

He goes on to philosophize, generally, about the pleasures of surprise: "nothing pleaseth but rare accidents." The followers of the older view of convention in Shakespeare (as represented by E. E. Stoll) would say that this is merely a warning to the audience not to judge Hal by his previous words and actions, as spectators in the theater are accustomed to do, but to wait until he reveals his true self. We will accordingly be in a conspiracy with the hero and enjoy a feeling of comic superiority towards the other characters, particularly Falstaff and Hal's father. Other critics, more in the train of A. C. Bradley than of Stoll, will take this speech to be relevant to Hal's character; *everything* he says and does on the stage is relevant, they say, and a character cannot step out of character. At any rate, here Prince Hal is not talking to himself or nobody. Rhetorically, he is addressing his absent comrades; it is an *apostrophe*, an address to something or someone, present or absent, which interrupts the surrounding discourse. But functionally, of course, he is talking to the theater audience.

The soliloquist par excellence who talks to himself is obviously Hamlet. How subjective and internal his thoughts are is emphasized in the final two lines of his first soliloquy:

> It is not, nor it cannot come to good,
> But break my heart, for I must hold my tongue.

$$\text{(I, ii, 158–59)}$$

He meditates on his own inaction, on being and non-being, on the nature of man. These latter themes are appropriate enough for sonnets, and this brings us to the consideration of the "audience" of the Shakespeare sonnets.

W. H. Auden thought that these are private poems, with no audience indicated or envisaged:

Though Shakespeare may have shown the sonnets to one or two intimate literary friends,—it would appear that he must have—he wrote them, I am quite certain, as one writes a diary, for himself alone, with no thought of a public.[5]

---

[5]*Signet Classic Shakespeare* edition (1964), p. xxxv. Stephen Spender agrees: "The sonnets are an intermittently-kept poetic diary covering a period, supposedly, of three years" (*The Riddle of Shakespeare's Sonnets* [1962], p. 95). But a few pages later (p. 100) he writes, "A thing that is often forgotten by writers about the sonnets is that they are not a monologue. They are one side of a dialogue, or a speech . . . or they are letters."

That this view is untenable will appear, I think, when we consider the question of the stated or implied addressee of the sonnets in groups and the rhetorical strategy of individual poems. Father Walter J. Ong has shown, in a notable paper, that "The Writer's Audience is Always a Fiction." In it he maintains that in the extreme case, the diary, the writer is not so simply addressing himself as one might think:

> The audience of the diarist is even more encased in fictions. What is easier, one might argue, than addressing oneself? As those who first begin a diary often find out, a great many things are easier. The reasons why are not hard to unearth. First of all, we do not normally talk to ourselves—certainly not in long, involved sentences and paragraphs. Second, the diarist pretending to be talking to himself has also, since he is writing, to pretend he is somehow not there. And to what self is he talking? To the self he imagines he is? Or would like to be? Or really thinks he is? Or thinks other people think he is? To himself as he is now? Or as he will probably be or ideally be twenty years hence? If he addresses not himself but "Dear Diary," who in the world is "Dear Diary"? What role does this imply? [6]

If it is true that even the diarist is addressing a *persona,* it must be even more true of the sonneteer, the poet who composes love poems. The audience exists, fictional or not, but it is not simple and it is not obvious.

Let us consider an example of Eliot's second of the three voices, Sonnet 87, a poem which is clearly addressed to another person, not a solitary meditation or soliloquy, but a message, rhetorically addressed to a recipient:

> Farewell, thou art too dear for my possessing,
> And like enough thou know'st thy estimate;
> The charter of thy worth gives thee releasing;
> My bonds in thee are all determinate.
> For how do I hold thee but by thy granting,
> And for that riches where is my deserving?
> The cause of this fair gift in me is wanting,
> And so my patent back again is swerving.
> Thyself thou gav'st, thy own worth then not knowing,
> Or me, to whom thou gav'st it, else mistaking,

So thy great gift, upon misprision growing,
Comes home again, on better judgment making.
Thus have I had thee as a dream doth flatter:
In sleep a king, but waking no such matter.

This is one of two sonnets with a feminine ending at every line. Taken by itself Sonnet 87 might be considered a metrical experiment and consequently of no great importance in content, but the other feminine-ending sonnet, 20, is notoriously significant: "A woman's face with Nature's own hand painted."

Number 87, addressed to a recipient, is peppered with personal pronouns: *my* (four times) and *thy* (six times); the vocabulary is that of technical legal possession and cost: *dear* (expensive), *possessing*, *estimate* (value), *charter*, *worth*, *releasing*, *bonds*, *granting*, *riches*, *gift*, *patent*, *worth* (again), and *gift* (again). A title for the poem might be "A Gift Recalled"—a subject which could have been handled as a meditation, a direct expression of grief at the loss of something valuable, but the presence of the person addressed is insisted upon, even into the concluding couplet:

Thus have I had *thee* as a dream doth flatter:
In sleep a king, but waking no such matter.

G. K. Hunter has made a distinction between the lyrical character and the dramatic character of the sonnets:

The power of these poems does not reside in lyrical utterance, the version they represent is an individual's, and to that extent like lyric, but in them the reader is not concerned with solitary imaginings presented as of universal significance (as in the odes of Keats and Shelley), but with the relation of one human heart to others. By setting up a system of tensions between forces presented as persons, Shakespeare's sonnets interest the reader in a manner akin to the dramatic.[7]

The sonnets which begin in the imperative mood obviously imply or evoke a listener, as in Sonnet 90:

---

[7] "The Dramatic Technique of Shakespeare's Sonnets," *Essays in Criticism* 3 (1953): 154. Hunter is discussing Sonnets 89 and 86.

6

> Then hate me when thou wilt, if ever, now,
> Now while the world is bent my deeds to cross,
> Join with the spite of fortune, make me bow, . . .

The vigor imparted by the imperative has evoked enthusiastic response from some critics. George Wyndham, for example, wrote, "I doubt if in all recorded speech such faultless perfection may be found, so sustained through fourteen consecutive lines."[8]

The first edition of the 154 sonnets, published by Thomas Thorpe in 1609, does not divide the poems into groups. Most modern critics do divide them; almost unanimously, they consider the first seventeen sonnets to be addressed to a young man, urging him to marry and beget children. Even editors who rearrange the order usually keep the first seventeen together. One of the most recent of the rearrangers, Brents Stirling, says, "There are no intrusions and no convincing signs of internal disarrangement. All sonnets of the group join to express a theme found nowhere else in the 1609 collection: the first fourteen urge a young man to father children that he may save his rare qualities from Time's ruin; the last three, 15–17, offer the poet's verse as a defense against Time only to question it as a means of preservation and to reassert fatherhood as Time's adversary."[9]

Nowhere else in Elizabethan sonneteering do we find this theme. In fact, urging a young man to marry and have offspring struck C. S. Lewis as an absurd pretext for writing the poems. "What man in the world," he asked, "except a father or a potential father-in-law, cares whether any other man gets married?"[10] The question, if meant seriously, shows a surprising ignorance of sixteenth-century attitudes. Erasmus wrote an elaborate epistle to persuade a young gentleman (neither his son nor his potential son-in-law) to marry. It is included in Thomas Wilson's *Arte of Rhetorique,* of which there were eight editions between 1553 and 1585. Sidney wrote a poem in which the old shepherd Geron advises the young shepherd Histor to marry.[11] In an emblem book, Otto van Veen's *Amorum Emblemata* (1608), dedicated

---

[8] *The Poems of Shakespeare* (1898), p. cxxxix.
[9] *The Shakespeare Sonnet Order: Poems and Groups* (1968), p. 45.
[10] *English Literature in the Sixteenth Century, Excluding Drama* (1959), p. 503.
[11] *Poems of Sir Philip Sidney,* ed. William Ringler (1962), p. 105, lines 70–81.

to "the most noble and incomparable pair of brethren" who were later to share the dedication of Shakespeare's First Folio, there is a poem containing many of the same arguments used in the first seventeen Shakespeare sonnets.[12] As J. W. Lever put it, the doctrine of Increase allowed Shakespeare "to express in the sonnet medium one of the most vital and comprehensive doctrines of the age."[13]

One of the seventeen sonnets usually considered a masterpiece is Number 12:

> When I do count the clock that tells the time,
> And see the brave day sunk in hideous night;
> When I behold the violet past prime,
> And sable curls [all] silver'd o'er with white;
> When lofty trees I see barren of leaves,
> Which erst from heat did canopy the herd,
> And summer's green all girded up in sheaves
> Borne on the bier with white and bristly beard;
> Then of thy beauty do I question make
> That thou among the wastes of time must go,
> Since sweets and beauties do themselves forsake,
> And die as fast as they see others grow,
>   And nothing 'gainst Time's scythe can make defense
>   Save breed, to brave him when he takes thee hence.

In the octave it is a meditation, the poet summoning up instances of the regrettable passage of time, speaking to himself as in 106 ("When in the chronicle of wasted time") and 30 ("When to the sessions of sweet silent thought"). In the sestet the young man is addressed, but fleetingly; he must go among the wastes of Time, and there is only his champion, Breed, to brave Time when he takes him thence. Characteristic Shakespearean motifs make their appearance—the hours of the day, the seasons of the year,[14] flowers and trees and harvest. Phrases from others in this little group of seventeen also give hints of the greatness of sonnets farther along in the collection: "the world's fresh

[12]Mario Praz, *Studies in Seventeenth Century Imagery* (1939), 1:104–07.
[13]*The Elizabethan Love Sonnet* (1956), p. 190.
[14]H. S. Donow's useful *Concordance to the Sonnet Sequences of Daniel, Drayton, Shakespeare, Sidney and Spenser* (1969) reveals the fact that Shakespeare refers to *Time, winter, summer, spring, autumn,* and *day* far more often than his fellow sonneteers. Sidney exceeds him in references to *night.*

ornament / And only herald to the gaudy spring" (1); "Thou art thy mother's glass, and she in thee / Calls back the lovely April of her prime" (3); "For never-resting time leads summer on / To hideous winter and confounds him there, / Sap check'd with frost and lusty leaves quite gone, / Beauty o'ersnow'd and bareness everywhere" (5).

As one reads through the first seventeen sonnets, he becomes aware of a second theme emerging from the shadow of the first ("From fairest creatures we desire increase"). It is the immortality of verse, an ancient topic, treated most eminently by Ovid and Horace, but more recently by poets of the Pléiade. Being celebrated in poetry is a way to immortality, even though for the poet (perhaps remembering his assignment) there is "a mightier way" (16.1), namely to have children. But 15, however it is nudged aside by 16, is one of the great ones:

> When I consider every thing that grows
> Holds in perfection but a little moment;
> That this huge stage presenteth nought but shows
> Whereon the stars in secret influence comment;
> When I perceive that men as plants increase,
> Cheerëd and check'd even by the self-same sky,
> Vaunt in their youthful sap, at height decrease,
> And wear their brave state out of memory:
> Then the conceit of this inconstant stay
> Sets you most rich in youth before my sight,
> Where wasteful Time debateth with Decay
> To change your day of youth to sullied night,
>   And all in war with Time for love of you,
>   As he takes from you, I ingraft you new.[15]

This sonnet begins as a reflective poem; it is not until line 10 that the young bachelor is addressed directly. So we overhear the meditation on "the conceit of this inconstant stay," but the dramatic turn in line 10 emphasizes the person addressed, with sounds chiming on the word *you: you, youth, your, youth, you, you, new.* The intrusion of the immortality of verse theme on the propagation theme is made more striking

---

[15]The sources of the imagery in the first eight lines have been traced to passages in La Primaudaye's *The French Academie* (1586) and to similar passages in Barnaby Googe's translation of Palingenius, *The Zodiake of Life* (1560 and later). The best discussion is in John Erskine Hankins, *Shakespeare's Derived Imagery* (1953), pp. 253–56.

by the return of the latter in the next sonnet, which is firmly linked to it:

> But wherefore do you not a mightier way
> Make war upon this bloody tyrant Time?

So far I have spoken of the propagation theme as an "assignment," though without specifying from whom. For all I know Shakespeare gave himself the assignment, for reasons beyond conjecture, but the generally held view is well expressed by Dover Wilson, who refers to the first seventeen sonnets as "a series of lovely poetical exercises, probably composed to order." [16] In a recent fascinating survey of the English sonnet sequences, however, Carol Thomas Neely has suggested that propagation is really a metaphor for writing poetry. She points out that Petrarch introduces the metaphor and that he is followed by Spenser when he writes "Unquiet thought, whom at the first I bred" in his second sonnet, and by Sidney in the first sonnet of *Astrophil and Stella:*

> Thus great with child to speak, and helpless in my throes,
> Biting my truant pen, beating myself for spite,
> "Fool," said my muse to me, "look in thy heart and write!"

"Shakespeare's opening sonnets to the young man," Neely writes, "urging him to beget a child, make this metaphor explicit by making it literal."

. . . But as the sequence progresses, another kind of procreation comes to supersede the first. . . . The verse is first seen as identical with, then superior to, the physical child. . . . The poetic begetting, however, must also be achieved by a kind of parthenogenesis since there seems little indication that love is generated in the youth. Shakespeare's opening sonnets manifest the sequence's underlying drive to breed and the way in which it is thwarted. The poet must do it by himself; he, and not the beloved, is the true 'onlie begetter' of the dedication. . . . In all of the sequences, as in Shakespeare's, parthenogenesis prevails; the poet-lover creates his desires, his beloved, his poetry, all out of his own head and comes to lament the barrenness of the enterprise. [17]

---

[16] *The New Shakespeare: The Sonnets,* ed. J. Dover Wilson (1966), p. 115.
[17] "The Structure of English Sonnet Sequences," *ELH* 45 (1978):365–67.

This suggestion is brilliant and stimulating to thought. I wish I could accept it. But I cannot, because I think Shakespeare keeps the child and the poetry separate, in the couplet to Sonnet 17, the conclusion to the series:

> But were some child of yours alive that time,
> You should live twice, in it, and in my rhyme.

That Sonnet 17 is the conclusion to the series is not perfectly evident to everyone. Some critics can admit that there are no further references to begetting of offspring in the remaining 137 sonnets without drawing any inferences from that fact. They are swayed by the awareness that the offspring theme has already been associated with immortality through verse, particularly in 15 and 17. They conclude that the young man of 1–17 is identical with the Fair Friend of 18–126. Stephen Booth, in his recent elaborate edition of the sonnets, comments, "Since a reader cannot be expected to know either that Sonnet 17 was the last of the sonnets in support of procreation or that Shakespeare is about to claim an immortality for his verse that the two preceding sonnets specifically question, line 12 [of Sonnet 18: "When in eternal lines to time thou grow'st"] will probably appear to lead into another exhortation to marry. The imperceptibility of the dividing line between the procreation sonnets and sonnets 18–126 is a primary reason for assuming that 1–126 all concern the same relationship."[18]

The dividing line is perceptible enough to me. There is little evidence in the first seventeen sonnets that the speaker feels love for the person addressed, or that he meditates to himself on the subject of love and is overheard. Beauty, yes, and its transitoriness, but not love. There is nothing like the conclusion of 19:

> Yet do thy worst, old Time: despite thy wrong,
> My love shall in my verse ever live young.

The concluding sonnet (as I take it) raises another question in its first line: "Who will believe my verse in time to come?". The question of the credibility of poetry is not an idle question. Sidney deals

---

[18]*Shakespeare's Sonnets* (1977), p. 162. The great weakness of Booth's edition, I think, is his total adherence to Empson's doctrine that *all* glosses are valid. See his edition, p. xiii.

with it seriously in his *Defense of Poetry*. He thinks it is particularly important in love poetry:

But truly many of such writings, as come under the banner of unresistable love, if I were a mistress would never persuade me they were in love, so coldly they apply fiery speeches,—as men that had rather read lovers' writings and so caught up certain swelling phrases, which hang together, like a man which once told my father that the wind was at northwest and by south, because he would be sure to name winds enough—than that in truth they feel those passions which easily (as I think) may be bewrayed by that same forcibleness or *energia* (as the Greeks call it) of the writer.[19]

It is important, then, that we consider the audience of the poem, fictional though it probably is, and respond appropriately. It is in this way, not merely by "overhearing," that we are able to judge the *energia* or forcibleness of the poem. Some sonnets of course are reflective, and some parts of sonnets are meditations which shift to the dramatic situation of the speaker-listener. In the propagation series, leading as it does into the celebration of the immortality of verse, we have a variety. Here it is well to return to the conclusion Eliot reaches in his essay on the three voices of poetry:

I think that in every poem, from the private meditation to the epic or drama, there is more than one voice to be heard. If the author never spoke to himself, the result would not be poetry, though it might be magnificent rhetoric; and part of our enjoyment of great poetry is the enjoyment of *overhearing* words which are not addressed to us. But if the poem were exclusively for the author, it would be a poem in a private and unknown language, and a poem which was a poem only for the author would not be a poem at all.[20]

[19]*Miscellaneous Prose of Sir Philip Sidney*, ed. Katherine Duncan-Jones and Jan Van Dorsten (1973), pp. 116–17.
[20]*On Poetry and Poets*, p. 109.

CHAPTER TWO

Personae

It has been said that in the first seventeen sonnets "Shakespeare wrote not so much as if he were in love himself, but as if he were trying to persuade a friend to love and marry; they describe, as it were from the outside, the fruits of love."[1] It has also been noticed by many readers that the first group of sonnets advocates prodigality, urges procreation, and tries to influence a young man about whom the reader can gather almost nothing except that he is a bachelor. He has no "character" or personality; he is physically beautiful and should therefore pass on that beauty to succeeding generations. Not to do so would be not only miserly but also a sin against nature and against the heritage he has from his ancestors.

The focus is very different in the sonnets numbered 18–126 in 1609. The Fair Friend is now the beloved of the speaker; he has a personality and a character. The sonnets express over and over again a moral concern about him. Prodigality is not encouraged, it is deplored. Great attention is paid to "inward worth" without neglecting "outward fair" (16.11). Even the conventional praise which promises to confer immortality is different. No longer is there a half-serious rivalry between a son and poetry to perpetuate the beauty of the young man. Poetry has won the contest; it is now the "mightier way" to make war upon that bloody tyrant, Time (16.1–2).

Sonnet 18 is fuller, more confident, more resonant than its comparable poem in the first series, "When I consider everything that grows" (15). It begins by displaying the speaker as "a poet whose art is the creation of metaphor."[2]

---

[1]John Russell Brown, *Shakespeare and His Comedies* (1957), p. 47.
[2]Anne Ferry, *All in War with Time* (1975), p. 10.

Shall I compare thee to a summer's day?
Thou art more lovely and more temperate:
Rough winds do shake the darling buds of May,
And summer's lease hath all too short a date;
Sometime too hot the eye of heaven shines,
And often is his gold complexion dimm'd,
And every fair from fair sometime declines,
By chance or nature's changing course untrimm'd:
But thy eternal summer shall not fade,
Nor lose possession of that fair thou ow'st,
Nor shall Death brag thou wand'rest in his shade,
When in eternal lines to time thou grow'st.
     So long as men can breathe or eyes can see,
     So long lives this, and this gives life to thee.

The promise of immortality through verse is a commonplace of classical and Renaissance poetry. But Shakespeare's use of the word "summer" drifts from the literal to the figurative in a very subtle way. When Titania, Queen of the Fairies, introduces herself to the transformed Bottom, she says

I am a spirit of no common rate;
The summer still doth tend upon my state;
And I do love thee, therefore go with me.

A Midsummer Night's Dream
(III, i, 154–56)

And the soliloquy which opens *Richard III* begins

Now is the winter of our discontent
Made glorious summer by this son of York.

The literal summer has its all too brief a time; its weather is sometimes too hot, or perhaps cloudy; but the Fair Friend's *eternal summer* shall not fade, or become less fair, or die, because poetry preserves it. In another mood, reflecting on the transience of beauty, Shakespeare calls the Fair Friend "beauty's summer" (104.14).

The most important thing about the Fair Friend addressed in the sonnets after 17 is that he is the perfect subject for poetry. He is more consistent, more reliable, more permanent than a summer's day because of the poetry about him. This brings the poet and the Fair

Friend into a far more intimate relationship than existed between the bachelor and the advocate of marriage in the first seventeen sonnets. As Rosalie Colie put it, "Clearly, the relation of poet to this friend is based on poetry; poetry is not only the conventional instrument of appeal to patron, friend, and lover, the conventional voice in beauty's praise; but poetry is also the poet himself, ingrained in his personality and thus marking (the dyer's hand) all his human realizations and relations."[3]

As a subject for poetry, the Fair Friend is inexhaustible. "How can my muse want subject to invent" asks Sonnet 38, "While thou dost breathe, that pour'st into my verse / Thine own sweet argument?" Sonnet 76 maintains that the poet has no other subject: "O know, sweet love, I always write of you, / And you and love are still [always] my argument." In Sonnet 79 the poet declares that the subject exceeds his poetic powers: "I grant, sweet love, thy lovely argument / Deserves the travail of a worthier pen." This modesty is traditional, and though it may seem inconsistent with the claims made for immortality through the poet's pen, readers of Shakespeare's sonnets (and indeed some parts of the plays) must be prepared to abandon logic when the occasion requires.

In other collections of Elizabethan sonnets, most of which can be called sequences with better justification than this one can, the beautiful person celebrated is a woman. Sometimes she is a real person; Sidney's Stella is Penelope Devereux, Lady Rich. Sometimes she is an invention, as Giles Fletcher's Licia is. Into which class the Fair Friend falls is quite uncertain. There have been many real persons suggested for the role, but all of these suggestions are wasted effort if, as is quite possible, the Fair Friend is an invention of the poet's. On this subject there is no certainty; the theories flare up and fade out, get lost among the shadows; the poetry remains.

It does matter, of course, what sort of figure the sonnets are addressed to—those which are clearly addressed to someone else, not to the poet himself and not to nobody. First of all, the Fair Friend has one quality in common with the heroines of Elizabethan sonnet cycles addressed to women: he is beautiful. But unlike the ladies of the other

---

[3]Rosalie Colie, *Shakespeare's Living Art* (1974), p. 66.

sonneteers, he loves the poet: Sonnet 25 contrasts the situation of the poet with that of people who can boast of public honor and proud titles, with great prince's favorites, with military heroes—all of whom may lose what they most enjoy.

> Then happy I that love and am beloved
> Where I may not remove, nor be removed.[4]

But the Fair Friend's beauty is not all external. He is said to have surpassing "worth" or virtue:

> Yet what of thee thy poet doth invent
> He robs thee of, and pays it thee again.
> He lends thee virtue, and he stole that word
> From thy behavior . . . .
>
> (79.7–10)

At times the poet has failed to do justice to his worth:

> And therefore have I slept in your report,
> That you yourself, being extant, well might show
> How far a modern quill doth come too short,
> Speaking of worth, what worth in you doth grow.
>
> (83.5–6)

Sometimes this worth or virtue is identified with constancy, which is, of course, natural enough in love poetry:

> In all external grace you have some part,
> But you like none, none you, for constant heart.
>
> (53.13–14)

A recent critic finds "worth" to signify something about poetry: "Throughout the sonnets, the paradox of poetry turns on the question of 'worth.' Even in his most disillusioned moods when thoughts of the world's corruption lead him to anticipate his own decay and death, Shakespeare never forgets the power of art to redeem life."[5] Finally, I

---

[4]In view of this couplet, I find J. B. Leishman's comment very strange: "Nowhere, one might almost say, in Shakespeare's sonnets is there unmistakable evidence that Shakespeare really believed that his friend, in any deep and meaningful sense of the word, really loved him at all. At most, perhaps, his friend 'quite liked him'." *Themes and Variations in Shakespeare's Sonnets* (1963), p. 226.

[5]John D. Bernard, " 'To Constancie Confin'de': The Poetics of Shakespeare's Sonnets," *PMLA* 94 (1979): 81.

think, "worth" is an aspect of love that is fundamentally mysterious, as in the proclamation that love is

> the star to every wand'ring bark
> Whose worth's unknown, although his highth be taken.
>
> (116.7–8)

The Fair Friend is younger than the poet: "My glass shall not persuade me I am old / So long as youth and thou are of one date / . . . . How can I then be elder than thou art?" (22.1–2, 8). He is of superior rank: "Lord of my love, to whom in vassalage / Thy merit hath my duty strongly knit" (26.1–2).

In fact, the poet is sometimes apprehensive that close association with him may cause social embarrassment or disgrace to the Fair Friend:

> I may not evermore acknowledge thee,
> Lest my bewailëd guilt should do thee shame,
> Nor thou with public kindness honor me,
> Unless thou take that honor from thy name.
>
> (36.9–12)

He carries this attitude to the extreme of warning the Fair Friend not to mourn for him after his death, lest the "wise world" mock him for caring about one so lowly (71 and 72).

Yet for all his "worth" and constancy, the Fair Friend is capable of snubbing the poet, of rejecting him as Prince Hal, newly become King Henry V, rejected his old crony Falstaff:

> Against that time when thou shalt strangely pass
> And scarcely greet me with that sun, thine eye,
> When love converted from the thing it was
> Shall reasons find of settled gravity. . .
>
> (49.5–8)

As M. M. Mahood says, this quatrain is "the rejection of Falstaff in little. The parallel is strengthened by the sun image (as in Hal's 'Yet herein will I imitate the sun') and by the way *gravity* calls to mind the Lord Chief Justice's reproach to Falstaff." She continues to characterize the Fair Friend as "a brilliant, prudent, calculating egotist."[6]

---

[6]M. M. Mahood, *Shakespeare's Wordplay* (1957), pp. 96, 98. Her essay, "Love's Confined Doom," in *Shakespeare Survey* 15 (1962): 50–61, is also very valuable.

17

Sonnet 87 ("Farewell, thou art too dear for my possessing"), which we have already discussed as a clear example of a sonnet addressed to someone, real or imaginary, is one of several in which the Fair Friend has rejected the poet or in some way broken with him. Sonnet 88, which begins

> When thou shalt be dispos'd to set me light,
> And place my merit in the eye of scorn,

promises casuistically that the speaker will take the side of the Fair Friend and so win glory because he indeed belongs to the Fair Friend. Sonnet 89 likewise embraces the reason why the poet has been abandoned:

> Say that thou didst forsake me for some fault,
> And I will comment upon that offense;

He will, he promises, side with the Fair Friend against himself:

> For thee, against myself I'll vow debate,
> For I must ne'er love him whom thou dost hate.

Sonnet 90 is closely linked, arguing that the Friend should hate him now, if ever, "Now while the world is bent my deeds to cross"; the Friend's abandonment should come first, in the vanguard of the other troubles, because in comparison the other troubles will then seem light.[7]

These sonnets have a common theme and they share the same rhetorical strategy. But just as, in the plays, dialogue may lead up to and prepare for a soliloquy, so these sonnets, addressed to a *persona,* can be viewed as preliminary to the meditative Sonnet 94, "They that have power to hurt and will do none." This sonnet generalizes; it is a "fearful meditation," connected of course with the commonplace, *optimae corruptio pessima.* But it should be understood as a reverie after the speeches of Sonnets 87, 88, 89, and 90 have been made.

What else do we know of the fault or the flaw of the Friend? Sonnets 33–35 portray it in a favorite Shakespearean metaphor, that of the

---

[7]This sonnet has been extravagantly praised. A writer in the *Times Literary Supplement* for December 11, 1924, p. 845, says that it "more and more asserts itself as the greatest of them all."

sun being obscured by clouds. It is used, we recall, by Prince Hal in his soliloquy notifying the audience that he will emerge from the cloud of dissipation now covering him and shine as a true prince should. Sonnet 33 is one of the most eloquent:

> Full many a glorious morning have I seen
> Flatter the mountain tops with sovereign eye,
> Kissing with golden face the meadows green,
> Gilding pale streams with heavenly alcumy,
> Anon permit the basest clouds to ride
> With ugly rack on his celestial face,
> And from the forlorn world his visage hide,
> Stealing unseen to west with this disgrace:
> Even so my sun one early morn did shine
> With all-triumphant splendor on my brow,
> But out, alack, he was but one hour mine,
> The region cloud hath mask'd him from me now.
>   Yet him for this my love no whit disdaineth:
>   Suns of the world may stain, when heaven's sun staineth.

The structure shows a clear division between octave and sestet. The sound texture is very rich, displaying alliteration and assonance not only within lines but across them. The movement is steady and regular, broken only by the exclamations in line 11. The rhyme words are firm and strong, modified by the feminine rhyme in the couplet. The sonnet is an example of a rhetorical figure which Puttenham describes as "the figure *Paradiastole*, which . . . we call the *Curry-favell*, as when we make the best of a bad thing . . . as, to call an unthrift, a liberall gentleman: the foolish-hardy, valiant or couragious: the niggard, thriftie . . . moderating and abating the force of the matter by craft, and for a pleasing purpose."[8]

Sonnet 34 is more severe, even though the Friend seems to have repented:

> Why didst thou promise such a beauteous day,
> And make me travel forth without my cloak,
> To let base clouds o'ertake me in my way,
> Hiding thy brav'ry in their rotten smoke?
> 'Tis not enough that through the cloud thou break,

---

[8] *The Arte of English Poesie*, ed. Willcock and Walker, pp. 62–63.

To dry the rain on my storm-beaten face,
For no man well of such a salve can speak
That heals the wound, and cures not the disgrace;
Nor can thy shame give physic to my grief,
Though thou repent, yet I have still the loss,
Th' offender's sorrow lends but weak relief
To him that bears the strong offense's [cross].
  Ah, but those tears are pearl which thy love sheeds,
  And they are rich, and ransom all ill deeds.

This is addressed directly to the Fair Friend, in contrast to the meditative Sonnet 33; it is full of personal pronouns. There is no structural division after line 8, though the imagery changes after line 6 from weather to medicine. However, there may be a link between the raindrops on the poet's face and the tears on the Friend's. The poem gains strength from a concentrated vocabulary including *disgrace, shame, grief, loss, sorrow,* and *cross.* The idea of a wound that could be cured by a salve but leaves a disgrace has led some editors to refer to Tarquin as he leaves Lucrece's bed:

Bearing away the wound that nothing healeth,
The scar that will despite of cure remain.

(731–32)

Sonnet 35, the last of the little series on the Friend's fault, continues the exculpation of the friend and accordingly is another *Curry-favell*, but it also confesses the casuistry of the poet, which the rhetorical figure *Paradiastole* was not supposed to do. This emphasis on the self consciousness of the poetry itself is very characteristic of Shakespeare, though it has baffled some of the critics and expositors:

No more be griev'd at that which thou hast done:
Roses have thorns, and silver fountains mud.
Clouds and eclipses stain both moon and sun,
And loathsome canker lives in sweetest bud.
All men make faults, and even I in this,
Authorizing thy trespass with compare,
Myself corrupting, salving thy amiss.
Excusing [thy] sins more than [thy] sins are;
For to thy sensual fault I bring in sense—
Thy adverse party is thy advocate—

And 'gainst myself a lawful plea commence.
Such civil war is in my love and hate
  That I an accessary needs must be
  To that sweet thief which sourly robs from me.

The opening words, "No more be griev'd" give us warning that platitudes are to follow, as in all attempts to offer consolation to a grieving person. A good example is Claudius' exhortation to Hamlet in I, ii, 87–117 of that play. The second quatrain involves the speaker in the fault making: it is a fault to justify a fault. From line 9 we learn that the Friend's fault was sensual, and the poet brings in "sense" or reason to justify it. (Malone's emendation "incense" is very ingenious but is not accepted by most editors because it is unnecessary and does not fit the court of law images in lines 9–11.) The identification of the fault as sensuality puts this sonnet into the company of Sonnets 40–42; in the first of these the Fair Friend is called "Lascivious grace, in whom all ill well shows," but these sonnets are apparently out of place in the 1609 order and seem to belong with the Dark Lady sonnets, to be discussed later. The couplet of Sonnet 93 is perhaps germane:

  How like Eve's apple doth thy beauty grow,
  If thy sweet virtue answer not thy show!

Sonnets 67 ("Ah, wherefore with infection should he live") and 68 ("Thus is his cheek the map of days outworn") accuse the Friend of artificiality and reflect the bias against cosmetics and extravagant dress which seems almost a personal trait of Shakespeare. But the following sonnets, 69 ("Those parts of thee that the world's eye doth view") and 70 ("That thou are blamed shall not be thy defect") are more specific about the Fair Friend and his reputation in the world. People who praise his beauty also look into his character:

  [Thy] outward thus with outward praise is crown'd,
  But those same tongues that give thee so thine own,
  In other accents do this praise confound
  By seeing farther than the eye hath shown.
  They look into the beauty of thy mind,
  And that in guess they measure by thy deeds,
  Then, churls, their thoughts (although their eyes were kind)
  To thy fair flower add the rank smell of weeds:

> But why thy odor matcheth not thy show,
> The [soil] is this, that thou dost common grow.
>
> (69.5–14)

[Soil] in line 14 is a generally accepted emendation for "solye" in the 1609 text. It means "solution" or "explanation," but puns on the commoner meaning, "stain, tarnish, blemish" as when Diomed, in *Troilus and Cressida,* in answer to the question who deserves Helen most, says

> He merits well to have her that doth seek her,
> Not making any scruple of her soil.
>
> (IV, i, 56–57)

Line 12 takes us back, quite directly, to Sonnet 94, with its reference to those who "rightly do inherit heaven's graces / And husband nature's riches from expense" and of course to the smell of weeds. Even more closely does it approach the two following sonnets, 95 ("How sweet and lovely dost thou make the shame") and 96 ("Some say thy fault is youth, some wantonness") whose first lines suffice to show the nature of the fault in the friend. From the poet's point of view, however, the fault is mainly important because it is the poet's business to defend and justify it.

Accordingly, we must now consider the character of the poet (or speaker) as it is revealed or hinted at in the sonnets. These are lyric poems, love poems associated in a loose way with two traditions, the Petrarchan love sonnet and the epigram tradition. They are not narrative poems. Their principal purpose, their reason for existence, is not to tell a story.

Since most of Shakespeare's work is dramatic, and the dramatist is hidden behind his characters, searchers for a clue to Shakespeare's personality have naturally turned to the sonnets. There they can find almost anything. Some, so literal-minded that their qualifications to read poetry seem very dubious, conclude from Sonnet 37.3, "So I, made lame by Fortune's dearest spite" that the poet suffered an injury to his leg. A more sophisticated recent commentator finds here a "dimly apparent" metaphor of sexual impotence.[9] Some literalists maintain that the two lines in Sonnet 111, "Whilst like a willing patient I will drink / Potions of eisel 'gainst my strong infection,"

---

[9]Stephen Booth, *Shakespeare's Sonnets* (1977), p. 195.

record that the poet was taking medicine to cure syphilis. But in actuality, the poet of the sonnets, the "I" who speaks the poems, is rather mysterious. As J. B. Leishman put it, "In the sonnets of our greatest dramatist, no less than in the sonnets of Petrarch, there is nothing that can properly be called 'self-dramatization'—not, at any rate, in the sense in which we so often have it in Ronsard, in Yeats, and in Donne."[10] Another critic makes the same point in different words: "The reason why the sonnets are the greatest love poems in the language is also the reason why Shakespeare is the greatest poetic dramatist. We could call it selflessness—and the critics have often drawn attention to the lack of self–assertion in Shakespeare's sonnets, compared to those of his contemporaries. We could borrow Keats's phrase and call it 'negative capability.' "[11]

I believe these critics are right in so far as their remarks apply to William Shakespeare, the author of the sonnets and the plays. But the "I" of the sonnets, though mysterious, is not quite so anonymous. He may or may not bear a close resemblance to William Shakespeare, but he is a *persona* with identifiable traits. The first is that he is a victim of circumstances and feels it strongly. Sonnet 29 displays the victim:

> When in disgrace with Fortune and men's eyes
> I all alone beweep my outcast state,
> And trouble deaf heaven with my bootless cries,
> And look upon myself and curse my fate,
> Wishing me like to one more rich in hope,
> Featur'd like him, like him with friends possess'd,
> Desiring this man's art and that man's scope,
> With what I most enjoy contented least;
> Yet in these thoughts myself almost despising,
> Haply I think on thee, and then my state
> (Like to the lark at break of day arising
> From sullen earth) sings hymns at heaven's gate,
>   For thy sweet love remcmb'red such wealth brings,
>   That then I scorn to change my state with kings.

The first quatrain expresses not only anguish at the speaker's misfortunes but irritation and boredom at the multiplicity of them. The

---

[10] *Themes and Variations* (1963), p. 69.
[11] Inga-Stina Ewbank in *A New Companion to Shakespeare Studies,* ed. Kenneth Muir and S. Schoenbaum (1971), p. 106.

lines move urgently, almost without caesura; the repeated *and* in lines 3 and 4 has the insistence of a drum beat. *Trouble* is much stronger as a verb than as a noun, and the assonance of *deaf heaven* as well as its semantic compression has a powerful effect.[12] The *one* in line 5 and the two *hims* of line 6 are three different people, as the addition of "*this* man's art" and "*that* man's scope" would seem to confirm. The pointing to five more fortunate men strengthens the force of *all alone* and *outcast* in line 2. The thought turns at the beginning of the sestet with *Yet,* and the image of the lark at heaven's gate (celebrated again, of course, in the great aubade in *Cymbeline* II, iii, 20–26) really portrays the speaker's spirit or mood, called *state* here but preparing for the double-meaning *state* ("condition" and "throne") in line 14. A very perceptive critic, Stanley Burnshaw, comments on this third quatrain, "The final figure, a small poem in itself, sweeps up with suddenness all that preceded. The speaker's 'state' is no longer compared with that of other people, as has been done up to this point; it *becomes* the lark singing hymns at the gate of heaven. 'Like' loses its force in the actualization of the image of soaring. The elements blend together in the new con-fusion that names a feeling which cannot be named by other means."[13] A distinguished musicologist once remarked that in the two uses of *state* Shakespeare was modulating from a minor to a major key.[14]

The contrast between the speaker and more successful or more prominent people is the basis of other sonnets. Sonnet 25 begins

> Let those who are in favor with their stars
> Of public honor and proud titles boast,
> Whilst I whom fortune of such triumph bars
> Unlook'd for joy in that I honor most.

Honor, the noun in line 2, has quite different associations from those of *honor* the verb in line 4. This sonnet, too, begins with a tone of complaint about obscurity and failure but almost immediately concludes

---

[12]I am aware of the fact that Kökeritz maintains that *heaven* and *haven* were homonyms: *Shakespeare's Pronunciation* (1953), p. 113. His evidence there is two puns, but puns need not be homophones. In his index of rhymes, p. 449, he rhymes *heaven* with *eaven, even.* See Sonnet 132.5, 7.

[13]*The Seamless Webb* (1970), pp. 89–90.

[14]W. H. Hadow, cited by W. G. Ingram and Theodore Redpath, *Shakespeare's Sonnets* (1965), p. 72.

with happiness. The poet does not really envy the court favorite who may lose his place in the sun at any moment, or the warrior who may lose all his honors and reputation after one defeat. His love is returned, and that is enough for him.

Sonnet 91 again makes the contrast:

> Some glory in their birth, some in their skill,
> Some in their wealth, some in their body's force,
> Some in their garments, though new-fangled ill,
> Some in their hawks and hounds, some in their horse;
> And every humor hath his adjunct pleasure,
> Wherein it finds a joy above the rest,
> But these particulars are not my measure,
> All these I better in one general best.
> Thy love is [better] than high birth to me,
> Richer than wealth, prouder than garments' cost,
> Of more delight than hawks or horses be,
> And having thee, of all men's pride I boast:
>> Wretched in this alone, that thou mayst take
>> All this away, and me most wretched make.

The reiteration of *Some* in the first quatrain gives an impression of a courtly world where everyone's own disposition leads him to pursue something worldly which gives him "a joy above the rest." But these are not for the speaker; they are not his "measure." (One can almost hear the silent rhyming "treasure.") The rhetorical trick in line 8 of playing *better* as a verb against *best* as a noun is followed by the triumph of *better* as a comparative adjective over *richer, prouder,* and *of more delight,* culminating in the "of all men's pride I boast," recalling the "Some glory" of the first line. Finally, by another verbal trick, *wretched* is used in two senses. In line 13 it means "deprived, unfulfilled" (Schmidt 2); in line 14 it means "miserable" (Schmidt 1).

In one of several sonnets apologizing for not expressing his love more fully, the speaker compares himself to an actor suffering from stage fright:

> As an unperfect actor on the stage
> Who with his fear is put besides his part . . .

(23.1–2)

Since Shakespeare himself was an actor, for part of his career anyway, and lived among actors for all of his years in London, it has been

25

tempting to identify the speaker with William Shakespeare the man. That he should use theater metaphors is natural enough. In the plays there are several memorable images. One is in the touching scene in *Coriolanus* when the hero's wife, mother, and son appeal to him not to destroy his country. He soliloquizes:

> Like a dull actor now
> I have forgot my part, and I am out,
> Even to a full disgrace.
>
> (V, iii, 40–42)

In *Richard II,* the Duke of York describes to his Duchess the entry of their two cousins, Bullingbrook and Richard, into London:

> As in a theatre the eyes of men,
> After a well-graced actor leaves the stage,
> Are idly bent on him that enters next,
> Thinking his prattle to be tedious . . .
>
> (V, ii, 23–26)

Leontes, in *The Winter's Tale,* thinks himself a cuckold and compares himself to an actor:

> Go play, boy, play. Thy mother plays, and I
> Play too, but so disgrac'd a part, whose issue
> Will hiss me to my grave . . .
>
> (I, ii, 187–89)

Finally, everyone knows the passage in which Macbeth cynically compares life itself to an actor:

> Life's but a walking shadow, a poor player
> That struts and frets his hour upon the stage
> And then is heard no more . . .
>
> (V, v, 24–26)

It is traditional to see references to Shakespeare's career as an actor in the little series 110–12, though surely something else is involved, too. Just what it is that the speaker is ashamed of is not made clear. Sonnet 110 begins as a rueful confession and ends with a promise of reform. This surely fits something bigger than an actor's life, however disreputable that might have seemed in some Elizabethan circles.

> Alas, 'tis true, I have gone here and there,
> And made myself a motley to the view,
> Gor'd mine own thoughts, sold cheap what is most dear,

Made old offenses of affections new;
Most true it is that I have look'd on truth
Askaunce and strangely: but by all above
These blenches gave my heart another youth,
And worse essays prov'd thee my best of love.
Now all is done, have what shall have no end,
Mine appetite I never more will grind
On newer proof, to try an older friend,
A god in love, to whom I am confin'd.
    Then give me welcome, next my heaven the best,
    Even to thy pure and most most loving breast.

The first three lines would fit the situation of a fastidious person making himself a mountebank on the stage, but by the time we have read through line 8 we feel that the behavior the speaker refers to must involve some kind of disloyalty in love. *Askaunce* means "with a sidelong glance, indifferently"; *blenches* means both "swervings away from constancy" and "blemishes." *Worse essays* means "experiments in what was inferior." The argument is that the speaker's infidelities have resulted in deeper love. It is important to remember that this is a "concession" sonnet, a traditional rhetorical form of which the most familiar example is probably Sidney's fifth sonnet in *Astrophil and Stella:*

It is most true, that eyes are form'd to serve
The inward light, and that the heavenly part
Ought to be king, from whose rules who do swerve,
Rebels to Nature, strive for their own smart. . .

It is in the very nature of the concession sonnet that more is conceded than need be.

Shakespeare's next sonnet belongs with 110 and adds to the impression that going here and there and making one's self a motley to the view are ways of describing what an actor does:

O, for my sake do you [with] Fortune chide,
The guilty goddess of my harmful deeds,
That did not better for my life provide
Than public means which public manners breeds.
Thence comes it that my name receives a brand,
And almost thence my nature is subdu'd

To what it works in, like the dyer's hand.
Pity me then, and wish I were renew'd,
Whilst like a willing patient I will drink
Potions of eisel 'gainst my strong infection,
No bitterness that I will bitter think,
Nor double penance, to correct correction.
    Pity me then, dear friend, and I assure ye,
    Even that your pity is enough to cure me.

This sonnet, though it has characteristic Shakespearean wordplay, assonance and alliteration, is peculiarly constructed. The turn of thought occurs after the seventh line; until then the subject is the soiling effect that public behavior has on the speaker's nature (Alexander Schmidt, in his authoritative *Shakespeare Lexicon,* defines this particular use of the word public as "vulgar"). In the following seven lines the disgrace is likened to a disease, which the speaker is willing to take any bitter medicine to cure. "Eisel" is vinegar, often taken to ward off the plague. Hamlet offers to drink it and eat a crocodile in the ranting contest with Laertes at Ophelia's grave (V, i, 276). Sonnet 111 persists in its medical figure, concluding in the couplet that the dear friend's pity would in itself be a complete remedy. The next sonnet, 112, speaks of a "vulgar scandal stamp'd upon my brow," which must be the same as the "brand" of 111. A "brand" is a mark of infamy, a stigma. The poet speaks on both sides of the matter; he is at once ashamed of the scandal and totally indifferent to the opinions of others, whether they are critics or flatterers. But it is in the tradition of sonnets that the paradox makes the poem.

If the sonnets dealing with the Friend's fault are largely casuistic and *Curry-favell,* pretending to defend the fault but really suffering from it, the sonnets on the *poet's* fault, 117–19, admit the guilt but argue that it leads to something better:

Accuse me thus: that I have scanted all
Wherein I should your great deserts repay,
Forgot upon your dearest love to call,
Whereto all bonds do tie me day by day;
That I have frequent been with unknown minds,
And given to time your own dear-purchas'd right;
That I have hoisted sail to all the winds
Which should transport me farthest from your sight.

28

Book both my willfulness and errors down,
And on just proof surmise accumulate;
Bring me within the level of your frown,
But shoot not at me in your wakened hate:
    Since my appeal says I did strive to prove
    The constancy and virtue of your love.

To be "frequent with unknown minds" is not very far, one would suppose, from the goring of one's own thoughts, selling cheap what is most dear, or looking at truth askaunce and strangely of Sonnet 110. But here the speaker does not promise to reform; instead he claims that these offenses were merely to test the friend's constancy. The general image of a court trial is interrupted by two quick images, of sailing in lines 7–8 and shooting in lines 11–12. Line 10 sounds obscure but Tucker Brooke paraphrases it "Pile on top of what you can prove all that you may suspect." "Level" means "target" or "field of fire," introducing the shooting image. Finally, "virtue" means "strength," not "goodness."

    There is a comparison of the two offenses, or rather of their effect upon the person offended, in Sonnet 120:

That you were once unkind befriends me now,
And for that sorrow which I then did feel
Needs must I under my transgression bow,
Unless my nerves were brass or hammered steel.
For if you were by my unkindness shaken
As I by yours, y'have pass'd a hell of time,
And I, a tyrant, have no leisure taken
To weigh how once I suffered in your crime.
O that our night of woe might have rememb'red
My deepest sense, how hard true sorrow hits,
And soon to you, as you to me then, tend'red
The humble salve which wounded bosoms fits!
    But that your trespass now becomes a fee,
    Mine ransoms yours, and yours must ransom me.

The "I" is very frank about the extent of his guilt:

To bitter sauces did I frame my feeding,
And sick of welfare, found a kind of meetness
To be diseas'd ere that there was true needing.

(118.6–8)

and again

> What potions I have drunk of Siren tears,
> Distill'd from limbecks foul as hell within,
> Applying fears to hopes, and hopes to fears,
> Still losing when I saw myself to win!

(119.1–4)

The identity of the poet's fault is left mysterious, as is the fault of the friend, but from its described effects and the imagery of food, disease, and wandering, one might well conclude that the offense was some kind of inconstancy. This is all the more apparent if we take the famous Sonnet 116 as an evocation of the opposite. The series 117–20 (or 121) is not, I think, a series of footnotes or attempts at parody of 116. These sonnets, which discuss the many facets of the vice of inconstancy, have their implied opposite—constancy. This is defined, both negatively and positively, in 116. For purposes of comprehension it is better to read it *after* the sonnets on the fault. What is Love, and what is it not?

> Let me not to the marriage of true minds
> Admit impediments; love is not love
> Which alters when it alteration finds,
> Or bends with the remover to remove.
> O no, it is an ever-fixëd mark
> That looks on tempests and is never shaken;
> It is the star to every wand'ring bark,
> Whose worth's unknown, although his highth be taken.
> Love's not Time's fool, though rosy lips and cheeks
> Within his bending sickle's compass come,
> Love alters not with his brief hours and weeks,
> But bears it out even to the edge of doom.
>   If this be error and upon me proved,
>   I never writ, nor no man ever loved.

This sonnet is justly a favorite. Its structure is clean and uncomplicated: three quatrains and a couplet, each quatrain beginning with a run-on line and ending with a strongly marked pause. The couplet rises to an almost defiant gesture, asserting again everything that has been said before. "Admit impediments" in line 2 invokes the marriage ceremony, and the tone and imagery of the first quatrain are rather formal and abstract. The second quatrain, with its images of a sea-mark

30

unshaken by tempests and the Pole star with its navigational integrity, is more concrete yet highly romantic. The third quatrain, on the superiority of love to Time, evokes images like those in Hotspur's dying speech:

> But thoughts, the slaves of life, and life, time's fool,
> And time, that takes survey of all the world,
> Must have a stop.

(1 Henry IV, V, iv, 81–83)

The marriage of true minds is the subject. Douglas Hamer has traced the theme back to an anonymous fifth-century Arian, then to a homily in the form of *Matrimonium non facit coitus, sed voluntas,* "Marriage is not made by the coition of two bodies, but by the union of two minds!" He relates this, usefully, to the union of Othello and Desdemona (I, iii, 252–65).[15]

The impression we get of the poet, then, varies from one of abject humility to serene confidence in the power of poetry and of love. He is also the poet of nature, of the seasons, of the emotions appropriate to them. There is a relationship between the poet and seasons which is even more significant than the comparison of the Fair Friend to a summer's day. The two lovely songs that conclude *Love's Labor's Lost* have little to do with the play but everything to do with Shakespeare. In Sonnet 97 absence from the loved one is compared to winter; the focus is on the feelings of the speaker, not the attributes of the one addressed:

> How like a winter hath my absence been
> From thee, the pleasure of the fleeting year!
> What freezings have I felt, what dark days seen!
> What old December's bareness everywhere!
> And yet this time remov'd was summer's time,
> The teeming autumn, big with rich increase,
> Bearing the wanton burthen of the prime,
> Like widowed wombs after their lords' decease:
> Yet this abundant issue seem'd to me
> But hope of orphans and unfathered fruit,
> For summer and his pleasures wait on thee,
> And thou away, the very birds are mute;

---

[15]*RES,* n.s. 25 (1974): 79–80.

> Or if they sing, 'tis with so dull a cheer
> That leaves look pale, dreading the winter's near.

The second and third quatrains are marked by turns of thought: "And yet," "Yet." The simple figure of weather as equivalent to emotions is developed into a complex one about reproduction in nature and in human beings. It was easier for an Elizabethan, especially Shakespeare, to think of agriculture and human growth in the same context. The couplet is particularly fine, following the third quatrain in meaning and rhyming with lines 2 and 4 of the first quatrain.

Both 97 and its companion, Sonnet 98, derive from Petrarch and his many imitators,[16] but they sound essentially Shakespearean and the insistence upon the first personal pronoun forces attention upon the role of the speaker:

> From you I have been absent in the spring,
> When proud-pied April, (dress'd in all his trim)
> Hath put a spirit of youth in every thing,
> That heavy Saturn laugh'd and leapt with him.
> Yet nor the lays of birds, nor the sweet smell
> Of different flowers in odor and in hue,
> Could make me any summer's story tell,
> Or from their proud lap pluck them where they grew;
> Nor did I wonder at the lily's white,
> Nor praise the deep vermilion in the rose,
> They were but sweet, but figures of delight,
> Drawn after you, you pattern of all those.
>   Yet seem'd it winter still, and, you away,
>   As with your shadow I with these did play.

Shakespeare says in Sonnet 14 "And yet methinks I have astronomy," and he uses it by bringing in Saturn, the planet which was supposed to shed gloom and sluggishness, but here laughs and leaps. "Summer's

---

[16]Leishman says "Indeed, perhaps no single one of Shakespeare's best sonnets can so profitably and so illuminatingly be compared with those of his predecessors; for nowhere more than in some of these sonnets written during an absence does he come so close to writing within an established convention, to accepting a traditional theme and situation, and yet in this, the finest of them, the differences from the sonnets of Petrarch, Ronsard and others on this theme are more striking than the resemblances" (*Themes and Variations*, p. 195).

story" is not just a narrative about summer, but a happy pleasant poem. *Summer* has become a symbol, and the flowers, which are invoked with all the charm of the nature songs in Shakespeare's plays, are, like the image or portrait of the absent Fair Friend, mere figures with which the poet can play.

In a larger sense, it is not seasons that occupy the poet's mind in the sonnets numbered 16–126; it is time itself, its ravages of beauty, its invulnerability, its all-encompassing power. In one sonnet, at least, Shakespeare turns specifically from the season theme to the larger theme of time. It is 65:

> Since brass, nor stone, nor earth, nor boundless sea,
> But sad mortality o'ersways their power,
> How with this rage shall beauty hold a plea,
> Whose action is no stronger than a flower?
> O how shall summer's honey breath hold out
> Against the wrackful siege of batt'ring days,
> When rocks impregnable are not so stout,
> Nor gates of steel so strong, but Time decays?
> O fearful meditation! where, alack,
> Shall Time's best jewel from Time's chest be hid?
> Or what strong hand can hold his swift foot back?
> Or who his spoil [of] beauty can forbid?
>   O none, unless this miracle have might,
>   That in black ink my love may still shine bright.

Some of the most eloquent sonnets in the collection are these "fearful meditations," reflecting upon the fragility and impermanence of beauty, of its transitory quality compared to such generally stable monuments as brass and stone. Sonnet 65 is almost a summary of such reflections, taken directly from passages in the fifteenth book of Ovid's *Metamorphoses* in the Arthur Golding translation. They also appear in Sonnets 55 ("Not marble nor the gilded [monuments] / Of princes"), 59 ("If there be nothing new, but that which is"), 60 ("Like as the waves make toward the pibbled shore"), 64 ("When I have seen by Time's fell hand defaced"). Minor problems of meaning occur in all of these. The "rage" in 65.3 means "violence," "destructive power," and line 10 is at first confusing until the reader sees that the meaning is "Where can the best jewel of all those from Time's chest be hidden from these thieving, destructive forces of Time?"

Aside from the permanence of poetry in comparison with other memorials, Ovid's *Metamorphoses* aroused in Shakespeare's mind questions about the passage of time—whether there had been deterioration, progress, or neither. The subject was an alive one in Shakespeare's time. The traditional view was of course that the best time was in the past. Spenser certainly thought so, though his friend Gabriel Harvey tried to persuade him that he should adopt the view of Jean Bodin, that the Golden Age was not in the past but in the future. Characteristically, Shakespeare seems not to have made up his mind. Sonnet 59 is illustrative:

> If there be nothing new, but that which is
> Hath been before, how are our brains beguil'd,
> Which laboring for invention bear amiss
> The second burthen of a former child!
> O that recórd could with a backward look,
> Even of five hundreth courses of the sun,
> Show me your image in some antique book,
> Since mind at first in character was done!
> That I might see what the old world could say
> To this composëd wonder of your frame,
> Whether we are mended, or whe'er better they,
> Or whether revolution be the same.
>   O, sure I am the wits of former days
>   To subjects worse have given admiring praise.

The claim for the immortality of verse in Ovid is the poet's own claim, but the philosophy of recurrence is Ovid's reporting of a long speech of Pythagoras. Aside from this Pythagorean theme in the sonnets, Shakespeare seems to have thought of the great philosopher only in comic contexts, and then only as the author of the idea that souls could transmigrate between animals and men. "Mind at first in character" means "Concepts first put down in handwriting." (Sonnet 108 begins "What's in the brain that ink may character.") "Frame" in line 10 means "form," and "mended" means "improved" in the next line.

The reference to "some antique book" in 59.7 relates to a sonnet in which that occupies the foreground, Number 106:

> When in the chronicle of wasted time
> I see descriptions of the fairest wights,

And beauty making beautiful old rhyme
In praise of ladies dead and lovely knights,
Then in the blazon of sweet beauty's best,
Of hand, of foot, of lip, of eye, of brow,
I see their antique pen would have express'd
Even such a beauty as you master now.
So all their praises are but prophecies
Of this our time, all you prefiguring,
And for they look'd but with divining eyes,
They had not still enough your worth to sing:
 For we, which now behold these present days
 Have eyes to wonder, but lack tongues to praise.

"Wasted" of course means bygone, but it carries also a suggestion that time is both capable of being wasted and of actively wasting people and things. "I wasted time, and now doth time waste me," says King Richard II (V, v, 49). The word "wights" was becoming archaic in Shakespeare's time, though it is common enough in Spenser. It occurs only here in the sonnets. There is a fine rhetorical trick in the third line, where "beauty making beautiful old rhyme" can mean either "the presence of the fairest wights making old rhyme, which would otherwise be uncouth and ugly, into beautiful verse" or "beauty (somehow identical with the poet or chronicler) making beautiful-old-rhyme," or both. Then there is a transferred adjective in line 4; the knights and ladies are both dead, but we would conventionally apply the adjective "lovely" to the ladies. The "blazon," originally a display of heraldic arms, is a catalog of beauties. Many Petrarchan sonnets are blazons; Shakespeare's Sonnet 130 ("My mistress' eyes are nothing like the sun") is an anti-blazon. We contemporaries may be poets but are not prophets; we *see* your actual beauty (and there is much emphasis on seeing in this sonnet) but it can only make us wonder; we cannot adequately praise it.

Emphasis on eyes and seeing leads to a consideration of the sonnets on sonnets. In Sonnet 114 the poet's eye is said to be the creative, image-making power:

 Or whether shall I say mine eye saith true,
 And that your love taught it this alcumy,
 To make of monsters and things indigest

35

> Such cherubins as your sweet self resemble,
> Creating every bad a perfect best
> As fast as objects to his beams assemble?
>
> (114.3–8)

Shakespeare likes the conceit of the eye as the transforming imagination of the poet. In one sonnet he equates it with painting:

> Mine eye hath play'd the painter and hath [stell'd]
> Thy beauty's form in table of my heart;
>
> (24.1–2)

In general *painting* is a pejorative word in the sonnets, especially when applied to methods other poets use in describing the Fair Friend. But first we must consider the sonnets which glance, directly or indirectly, at the nature of poetry itself. Poetry cannot easily be separated from love in the sonnets, to be sure, and since they both have intimate connections with the person addressed, these may be considered to be poems to be heard, not overheard. Several sonnets are specific about the Fair Friend as the "argument" or subject matter of the sonnets. That is what saves them, if we are to believe the poet. Sonnets 38, 76, and 79 share this theme:

> How can my Muse want subject to invent
> While thou dost breathe, that pour'st into my verse
> Thine own sweet argument, too excellent
> For every vulgar paper to rehearse?

and, more directly to the addressee:

> O know, sweet love, I always write of you,
> And you and love are still my argument.
>
> (76.9–10)

Sometimes the poet professes a (true or false?) modesty as a celebrant of the subject:

> I grant, sweet love, thy lovely argument
> Deserves the travail of a worthier pen.[17]
>
> (79.5–6)

---

[17]Schmidt gives a host of examples of meaning 3 for *argument:* "the theme, the subject," and I believe this is the primary, if not the sole, meaning of the word in the sonnets quoted here. Booth, in his edition, tries to insinuate a sexual meaning for the word, even when, in the context, it makes nonsense. He is misled, I think, by

A traditional claim of the Petrarchan sonneteer is that his verse is
plain, unaffected, and sincere whereas other poets are guilty of false ornament, elaboration, fancy use of mythology and extravagant exaggeration which renders their entire claim suspect. Such a sonnet is
Shakespeare's 21:

> So is it not with me as with that Muse
> Stirr'd by a painted beauty to his verse,
> Who heaven itself for ornament doth use,
> And every fair with his fair doth rehearse,
> Making a couplement of proud compare
> With sun and moon, with earth and sea's rich gems,
> With April's first-born flowers, and all things rare
> That heaven's air in this huge rondure hems.
> O, let me, true in love, but truly write,
> And then believe me, my love is as fair
> As any mother's child, though not so bright
> As those gold candles fix'd in heaven's air:
>> Let them say more that like of hearsay well,
>> I will not praise that purpose not to sell.

That the protests made here are part of the convention may be seen by
reading Sidney's sonnets 1 ("Loving in truth, and fain in verse my
love to show"); 3 ("Let dainty wits cry on the sisters nine"); 15 ("You
that do search for every purling spring") and possibly 6 ("Some lovers
speak when they their muses entertain"). Sonneteers in the Petrarchan
tradition utilize the clichés of that tradition, but, like DuBellay in
France, they scoff at other Petrarchists.[18]

A series of sonnets, numbered 76–86 in the 1609 order, concerns
itself with poetry, the one interruption being Sonnet 77, apparently a
note to accompany the gift of a blank book. In this series we get a tone
far different from that of the "immortalizing" sonnets. It involves
other poets and the contrast between the speaker and them. Of course

Farmer's definition of the French *l'argument* and by Ellis's citing of *T & C* IV, v, 26–
29 and *R & J* II, iv, 94–96. The kissing scene in *Troilus and Cressida* uses the word in
several senses, all in Schmidt. The *Romeo and Juliet* passage is part of Mercutio's
bawdry; it is characteristic of him that he can give a dirty meaning to any word. The
poet of the sonnets is no Mercutio. When he wishes to be indecent, as he does in
Sonnets 20, 135, and 151, he makes it perfectly clear.

[18]See Anne Lake Prescott, *French Poets and the English Renaissance* (1978), chap. 2.

Sidney had referred to other poets, but he challenged their artificial style, their lack of *energia,* and he was complacent about the alleged simplicity and sincerity of his own verse. Sidney never considers himself inferior in any way to the others—quite the contrary. Shakespeare, on the other hand, yields to his rivals. Sonnet 80 is perhaps the best example:

> O how I faint when I of you do write,
> Knowing a better spirit doth use your name,
> And in the praise thereof spends all his might,
> To make me tongue-tied, speaking of your fame.
> But since your worth (wide as the ocean is)
> The humble as the proudest sail doth bear,
> My saucy bark (inferior far to his)
> On your broad main doth wilfully appear.
> Your shallowest help will hold me up afloat,
> Whilst he upon your soundless deep doth ride,
> Or (being wrack'd) I am a worthless boat,
> He of tall building and of goodly pride.
> > Then if he thrive and I be cast away,
> > The worst was this: my love was my decay.

Here the rivals have been reduced to one, although in Sonnet 78 the reference is to "every alien pen." The implication to some commentators on line 9 is that the poem is addressed to a patron; why else would the poet refer to the slightest ("shallowest") help? Shakespeare treats the poet-patron relationship incidentally in *Timon of Athens,* and of course the dedications of *Venus and Adonis* and *Lucrece* to Southampton cannot be forgotten. But the Rival Poet has exercised the ingenuity and imagination of readers as much as the identity of the Fair Friend and the Dark Lady. The sonnet which seems to have given the most clues to the amateur detectives is 86:

> Was it the proud full sail of his great verse,
> Bound for the prize of all-too-precious you,
> That did my ripe thoughts in my brain inhearse,
> Making their tomb the womb wherein they grew?
> Was it his spirit, by spirits taught to write
> Above a mortal pitch, that struck me dead?
> No, neither he, nor his compeers by night
> Giving him aid, my verse astonishëd.

38

He, nor that affable familiar ghost
Which nightly gulls him with intelligence,
As victors of my silence cannot boast;
I was not sick of any fear from thence:
But when your countenance fill'd up his line,
Then lack'd I matter, that enfeebled mine.

There have been supporters of Marlowe, Chapman, Daniel, Barnes, and many other versifiers of the period, but Hyder Rollins, after surveying the field, dismissed them all as contributions to the chronicle of wasted time.[19] Though not the first, Rosalie Colie is a recent and interesting exponent of the idea that Shakespeare invented the Rival Poet:

That Shakespeare has provided poetic theory with a body and a personality in the fictive Rival Poet, around whom he organized a drama of verse and about verse, thereby invigorating an entirely academic convention of sonnet metamorphosis, is less surprising than that he thereby intensifies and dramatizes recurrent questions of styles—of praise, of imitation, of self-projection. The Rival Poet is invoked not as a voice for "style" of verse simply, though he unquestionably is made into a topic for discussing that subject. Because in this poet's prodigal economy, verse so clearly *is* the man, and a chosen style so interpenetrated with its poet's personality, the Rival Poet becomes an animate, breathing threat to our poet's continued life as poet, as friend, as man, a threat which can only be warded off by a purified rededication to poetic integrity.[20]

The ten sonnets preceding 86 all have to do with the ways in which poets can praise their loves; there is nothing strikingly original about Shakespeare's handling of this theme, but there are some characteristic ironies in such passages as

The dedicated words which writers use
Of their fair subject, blessing every book

(82.3–4)

and

I found (or thought I found) you did exceed
The barren tender of a poet's debt

(83.3–4)

[19] *The Variorum Shakespeare: The Sonnets* (1944), 2:294.
[20] *Shakespeare's Living Art* (1974), pp. 66–67.

39

as well as

> While comments of your praise, richly compil'd,
> Reserve their character with golden quill
> And precious phrase by all the Muses fil'd.
>
> (85.2-4)

This ironic tone is the counterpart of the sonorous and eloquent boasts about the immortalizing power of the sonnets themselves, one of which creeps into this series:

> Your name from hence immortal life shall have,
> Though I (once gone) to all the world must die;
> The earth can yield me but a common grave,
> When you entombëd in men's eyes shall lie;
> Your monument shall be my gentle verse,
> Which eyes not yet created shall o'er-read,
> And tongues to be your being shall rehearse,
> When all the breathers of this world are dead;
>
> (81.5-10)

For comparison, one may recall some lines of Samuel Daniel, occasionally favored as the Rival Poet, on the future of Elizabethan poetry:

> And who, in time, knows whither we may vent
> The treasure of our tongue, to what strange shores
> This gain of our best glory shall be sent
> T'enrich unknowing nations with our stores?
> What worlds in th'yet unformëd occident
> May come refin'd with th'accents that are ours.[21]

Whether in praise of the Fair Friend, or in complaint about his fault, or in justification of the poet's own shortcomings, the sonnets numbered 18-126 in the 1609 edition constitute an unrivaled masterwork. They are love poetry beyond what was considered love poetry by the Petrarchan sonneteers. Some are philosophical poems, meditations on the conflict between Time and ephemeral beauty, or between monuments of marble and immortal verse. Some are celebrations of the intimate relationship between the seasons of the year and human emotions. They are, often, ingenious exercises in wit—verbal, rhetorical, logical. They are not, I think, in any way poems meant to be

---

[21] *Musophilus*, ed. Raymond Himelick (1965), ll. 957-62.

"overheard." They speak, most of the time, to a *persona,* perhaps invented, perhaps derived in some way from an actual person. They are lyric poems, expressing mainly feelings that any capable reader can respond to as profound and true. But they are poems of the second voice, poems addressed to an audience of one or more, poems to be heard and mentally responded to. They are, for the most part, not soliloquies, or overheard poems. They derive some force from this fact. The persona of the hearer enables the reader to participate in the poem in a more active way than is possible for the overhearer. The poem is not quite dialogue but it is closer to dialogue than to soliloquy. This is the kind of poem that only a dramatist could write. Even in the compass of the sonnets, all the world's a stage.

> ### 126
> O Thou my louely Boy who in thy power,
>   Doeſt hould times fickle glaſſe.his fickle,hower:
> Who haſt by wayning growne,and therein ſhou'ſt,
> Thy louers withering,as thy ſweet ſelfe grow'ſt.
> If Nature(ſoueraine miſteres ouer wrack)
> As thou goeſt onwards ſtill will plucke thee backe,
> She keepes thee to this purpoſe,that her skill.
> May time diſgrace,and wretched mynuit kill.
> Yet feare her O thou minnion of her pleaſure,
> She may detaine,but not ſtill keepe her treſurel
> Her *Audite*(though delayd)anſwer'd muſt be,
> And her *Quietus* is to render thee.
>   (   )
>   (   )

CHAPTER THREE

The Poet and the World

In the series of poems to, or about, the Fair Friend, it is clear that the enemy is Time:

> reckoning Time, whose million'd accidents
> Creep in 'twixt vows, and change decrees of kings,
> Tan sacred beauty, blunt the sharp'st intents,
> Divert strong minds to th' course of alt'ring things
>
> (115.5–8)

but there is also an awareness that the love celebrated exists in an environment, that is to say a world outside the relationship. Is that world friendly, indifferent, or hostile? Is it even identifiable as court, city or country? What are its characteristics? Sonnet 124 seems to identify the world as the world of public affairs as contrasted with the private world of the lovers:

> If my dear love were but the child of state,
> It might for Fortune's bastard be unfather'd,
> As subject to Time's love, or to Time's hate,
> Weeds among weeds, or flowers with flowers gather'd.
> No, it was builded far from accident;
> It suffers not in smiling pomp, nor falls
> Under the blow of thrallèd discontent,
> Whereto th'inviting time our fashion calls;
> It fears not policy, that heretic,
> Which works on leases of short-numb'red hours,
> But all alone stands hugely politic,
> That it nor grows with heat, nor drowns with show'rs.
>   To this I witness call the fools of Time,
>   Which die for goodness, who have liv'd for crime.

In the first line *love* is the feeling, not the person beloved, despite the adjective *dear*. Often enough the term is personified, as in "Dear my

43

love, you know you had a father" (13.13); or "After my death, dear love, forget me quite" (72.3). But here the pronoun *it* which begins line 2 depersonifies any suggestions from *dear* to *child* in line 1; almost immediately, however, *love* is personified again by development of the *child of state* image. A child of state might be a bastard, Fortune's bastard, without a legal father. It might be subject to the fickleness of Time, which alternately loves and hates, or be gathered at random, a weed among weeds or a flower among flowers.

The second quatrain starts emphatically, with a *No*. It is not insecure as courtiers are, changing from *smiling pomp* to *thrallèd discontent*. Inviting time and fashion have a courtly touch. The third quatrain plays on the ambiguous word *policy,* which can mean "prudent wisdom in the management of public or private concerns" (Schmidt 3) but must have at least a shade of the meaning "cunning or strategem" (Schmidt 4), since it is called *that heretic.* Plain dealing is apparently orthodoxy. *Policy* is vacillating; it works on *leases of short-numb'red hours.* The speaker's love stands all alone, *hugely politic,* where the adjective picks up connotations of "prudent, wise" and remains impervious to weather: *nor grows with heat, nor drowns with showers.* (*Showers* in Shakespeare means "downpours.")

The quatrains are full of opposites (*child of state, Fortune's bastard*) (hated or loved by time), (*weeds, flowers*), (*smiling pomp, thrallèd discontent*), (temporary, permanent). So, in the couplet, which is of the proof-challenge type, as in "If this be error, and upon me proved, / I never writ, nor no man ever loved" (116), the *fools of time* are time servers and they lead paradoxical lives: they die for goodness who have lived for crime. Calling them as witnesses is ironic, though in their folly and subservience they may have learned, in the hard way, that love alone is hugely politic. These witnesses are presumably identical with the dwellers on form and favor of Sonnet 125.5.[1]

There are, then, some sonnets that reflect a concern about the world, as distinguished from Time or Fortune. These opponents may operate together, as they seem to do in Sonnet 90:

[1]This sonnet has puzzled the critics. Landry says it "is perhaps the most difficult of all the sonnets to interpret in detail" (*Interpretations in Shakespeare's Sonnets,* 1963, p. 113), and Booth calls it "the most extreme example of Shakespeare's constructive vagueness" (*Shakespeare's Sonnets,* 1977, p. 479). Arther Mizener's explication in "The Structure of Figurative Language in Shakespeare's Sonnets" in Barbara Herrnstein, *Discussions of Shakespeare's Sonnets* is perhaps the most ambitious.

Then hate me when thou wilt, if ever, now,
Now while the world is bent my deeds to cross,
Join with the spite of Fortune, make me bow,

yet in the sonnets after 126 there seems to be a more jaded view of "the
world," a greater consciousness of it. In Sonnet 112 the poet could say
to the Fair Friend "You are all my world . . ." but this assurance is
missing in the Dark Lady series; it is more common to encounter such
lines as

> Unlearnèd in the world's false subtilties   (138.4)

or

> All this the world well knows, yet none knows well   (129.13)

or

> Now this ill-wresting world is grown so bad   (140.11)

Sonnet 66, to be sure, offers a catalog of what is wrong with the
world. It, like 124, is a meditative sonnet, not addressed to the Fair
Friend, but rather to the poet himself:

> Tir'd with all these, for restful death I cry:
> As to behold desert a beggar born,
> And needy nothing trimm'd in jollity,
> And purest faith unhappily forsworn,
> And gilded honor shamefully misplac'd,
> And maiden virtue rudely strumpeted,
> And right perfection wrongfully disgrac'd,
> And strength by limping sway disablèd,
> And art made tongue-tied by authority,
> And folly (doctor-like) controlling skill,
> And simple truth miscall'd simplicity,
> And captive good attending captain ill:
> > Tir'd with all these, from these I would be gone,
> > Save that to die, I leave my love alone.

This is a very harmonious litany. The first line begins with an assonance (*Tir'd, cry*) and has an internal one (*rest-death*). Its scansion, to
the caesura, is not iambic. Line 2 almost hunts the letter (*behold, beggar, born*), while the next line pairs *needy* and *nothing* and line 4 follows

45

with *faith* and *forsworn*. The second quatrain follows the pattern of line 4 in ending with an adverb preceding a past participle (*unhappily forsworn, shamefully misplac'd, rudely strumpeted, wrongfully disgrac'd*), and the damnable iteration is reinforced by the insistent *and* beginning each line. But the last line of the quatrain changes the pattern: until line 12 all the abused qualities are abstractions (*desert, needy nothing, faith, honor, virtue, perfection, strength, art*). Toward the end we get iconographic figures, reminiscent of the woodcuts in an emblem book: *limping sway, captive good, captain ill*. The first line of the couplet repeats the exclamatory opening of the sonnet, but where the first line, after the caesura, has *for*—approaching something, the couplet has *from*—leaving something. The first line has the Keatsian *restful death*, which is approachable; the last line has the ominous, alliterative music of a departure: "Save that to die, I leave my love alone."

The world seen in Shakespeare's sonnets is by and large a courtly world. One first experiences a shock of surprise when he encounters the opening of Sonnet 143, with its homely barnyard imagery:

> Lo as a careful huswife runs to catch
> One of her feathered creatures broke away,
> Sets down her babe and makes all swift dispatch
> In pursuit of the thing she would have stay. . . .[2]

143

LOe as a carefull huswife runnes to catch,
One of her fethered creatures broake away,
Sets downe her babe and makes all swift dispatch
In pursuit of the thing she would haue stay:
Whilst her neglected child holds her in chace,
Cries to catch her whose busie care is bent,
To follow that which flies before her face:
Not prizing her poore infants discontent;
So runst thou after that which flies from thee,
Whilst I thy babe chace thee a farre behind,
But if thou catch thy hope turne back to me:
And play the mothers part kisse me, be kind.
  So will I pray that thou maist haue thy *Will*,
  If thou turne back and my loude crying still.

[2]One critic actually takes the *feathered creature* to be a courtier.

The significance of this point about the "world" is that it is courtly and the passages in Shakespeare's plays that represent a reaction to sexual depravity are scenes with a courtly background. King Lear's fulminations about sex may be a madman's ravings, but they strike home:

> But to the girdle do the gods inherit,
> Beneath is all the fiends'; there's hell, there's darkness,
> There is the sulphurous pit, burning, scalding,
> Stench, consumption. . .
>
> (IV, vi, 126–29)

and another king, Claudius, exclaims

> The harlot's cheek, beautied with plast'ring art,
> Is not more ugly to the thing that helps it
> Than is my deed to my most painted word.
>
> (III, i, 50–52)

Even Marina, in the brothel, is visited by the ruler of the country, who is sensitive to appeals to his honor (*Pericles* IV, vi). Philip Edwards sees a connection here: "What we have read in the sonnets helps us to explain the chiaroscuro of Marina in the brothel."[3] I should put it the other way around: we shall understand the Dark Lady sonnets better if we bring to their reading the appropriate passages in the plays.

The real difficulty about the Dark Lady sonnets is to decide the order in which they should be read. The 1609 order has been attacked and defended. But many readers have felt that Sonnets 40–42 refer to the same situation as in some sonnets after 126, and that they were misplaced because they are addressed to the Fair Friend instead of to the Dark Lady.

If the sonnets after 126 were arranged in a systematic and logical order, one would expect 144 ("Two loves I have of comfort and despair") to begin the Dark Lady series. But instead 127 leads off, confining itself almost entirely to the brunette beauty of the lady:

> In the old age black was not counted fair,
> Or if it were it bore not beauty's name;
> But now is black beauty's successive heir,
> And beauty slander'd with a bastard shame,

---

[3] *Shakespeare and the Confines of Art* (1968), p. 30.

For since each hand hath put on nature's power,
Fairing the foul with art's false borrow'd face,
Sweet beauty hath no name, no holy bow'r,
But is profan'd, if not lives in disgrace.
Therefore my mistress' eyes are raven black,
Their brows so suited as they mourners seem
At such who, not born fair, no beauty lack,
Sland'ring creation with a false esteem:
    Yet so they mourn, becoming of their woe,
    That every tongue says beauty should look so.[4]

Beauty in the first quatrain is blonde; it is displaced by *black,* the legitimate heir, and blonde beauty is declared a bastard. This invokes some of the same imagery and thought we noticed in 124. It is also remarkably reminiscent of Shakespeare's handling of blackness in *Love's Labor's Lost:* Berowne says, in defending Rosaline's beauty against the slurs of the King:

Devils soonest tempt, resembling spirits of light.
O, if in black my lady's brows be deck'd,
It mourns that painting [and] usurping hair
Should ravish doters with a false aspect:
And therefore is she born to make black fair.

                                    (IV, iii, 253–57)

Sonnets 130, 131, and 132 all refer again to the dark eyes, and the latter poem elaborates on the idea:

Thine eyes I love, and they as pitying me,
Knowing thy heart torment me with disdain,
Have put on black, and loving mourners be,
Looking with pretty ruth upon my pain.

Sidney's Stella has black eyes, as did her original, Penelope Rich, and Sidney develops several conceits on their color in *Astrophil and Stella* 7 and 9. This violation of the standard praise of blonde beauty as the only true beauty was in fact part of the tradition.[5]

---

[4] I have accepted emendations of *Her eyes* to *Their brows* and *and* to *as* in line 10.
[5] The following plea is a part of *A Woman's Woorth,* 1599 (STC 11831), fols. 56ᵛ–57:

"But tell me, will not you iudge the woman to bee moste fayre, that writte to her Louer in thys manner?

    My Loue, I am a little blacke,
    But say that I were much more blacke.

Shakespeare's Sonnet 131, however, adds a further meaning to the idea of blackness:

Thou art as tyrannous, so as thou art,
As those whose beauties proudly make them cruel;
For well thou know'st to my dear doting heart
Thou art the fairest and most precious jewel.
Yet in good faith some say that thee behold,
Thy face hath not the power to make love groan;
To say they err I dare not be so bold,
Although I swear it to myself alone.
And to be sure that is not false I swear,
A thousand groans, but thinking on thy face,
One on another's neck, do witness bear
That black is fairest in my judgment's place.

Mine eyes browne, my face like browne,
Admit my necke and brests more browne.
My haire and skin all black to be,
Sauing my teeth of Iuory:
Inuironed with a curroll fence,
Which breaths more sweet then frankinsense
That might delight both Gods and men,
Much more thyselfe, what saist thou then?
Must I for this my louely browne,
Haue my Loue on me to frowne?
Are not mine eyes as piercing still,
And able Marble hearts to kill?
Or can my Loue be ere the lesse,
My minde being made of gentlenesse?
Why night is duskie, sable blacke,
Yet no beautious starres doe lecke;
When the Moone with siluer light,
Gallops through the thicke fac'd night,
Venus doth loue nights brownest howers,
The darkest nookes are her safe bowers,
Thickets and Forrestes most obscure.
Yea, where no haunt hath been in ure,
Thither doth she most repayre,
Sooner then to a garden faire.
There may be seene the liuely sparke,
Thats best discerned in the darke:
The ball that in a bright blacke eye,
Shines like a Meteor in the skie.
There browne and faire are both as one,
When two sweet soules are so alone:
Tell me then (Loue) in such a night,
Wouldst thou not thinke the brownest white?"

49

In nothing art thou black save in thy deeds,
And thence this slander as I think proceeds.

It is not a profound poem, so it is rather easily paraphrased: You are as tyrannous as those conventional proud beauties, because to me you are the most precious and most beautiful. Other people say you are not so beautiful; I don't contradict them, except to myself. To be sure I am not lying, I groan a thousand times consecutively, thinking of your face.[6] This proves I am right: your actions, not your looks, are black. This is why people say "Thy face hath not the power to make love groan." But here black has not remained a color; it has become synonymous with evil, moral corruption, perhaps unbridled sexuality.

The conflict between eye and heart which is the theme of many sonnets is elaborated in Sonnet 141:

In faith, I do not love thee with mine eyes,
For they in thee a thousand errors note,
But 'tis my heart that loves what they despise,
Who in despite of view is pleas'd to dote;
Nor are mine ears with thy tongue's tune delighted,
Nor tender feeling to base touches prone,
Nor taste, nor smell, desire to be invited
To any sensual feast with thee alone;
But my five wits nor my five senses can
Dissuade one foolish heart from serving thee,
Who leaves unsway'd the likeness of a man,
Thy proud heart's slave and vassal wretch to be.
　　Only my plague thus far I count my gain,
　　That she that makes me sin awards me pain.

"In despite of view" means "despite what they (my eyes) see"; there is a word play between "despite" and "despise" here. "Dote" means to love excessively, as in the first lines of *Antony and Cleopatra*:

Phi. Nay, but this dotage of our general's
O'erflows the measure. Those his goodly eyes,
That o'er the files and musters of the war

---

[6]Cf. *Romeo and Juliet* I, i, 199–200:
Ben. Tell me in sadness, who is that you love?
Rom. What, shall I groan and tell thee?

Have glow'd like plated Mars, now bend, now turn
The office and devotion of their view
Upon a tawny front. . .

(I, i, 1–6)

The Dark Lady, unlike the Fair Friend, does not have a seductive
voice. (Sonnet 8 addresses the Fair Friend "Music to hear, why hear'st
thou music sadly?".) In fact, it seems, neither the five wits (intellec-
tual faculties) nor the five senses authorize the speaker's love; it comes
entirely from the foolish heart, or what will be called "will." He is the
mere "likeness of a man" because his heart has left his body to become
the "slave and vassal wretch" of the Dark Lady. His only consolation
is that he is suffering some of the pain for his sin which later might be
inflicted as punishment.

The *plague* spoken of here (and we should remember that the Elizabethans would read the word in a less figurative sense than we do)
reappears in the couplet of Sonnet 137; this poem also makes clear that
the moral blackness of the Dark Lady is promiscuity:

Thou blind fool, Love, what does thou to mine eyes,
That they behold and see not what they see?
They know what beauty is, see where it lies,
Yet what the best is take the worst to be.
If eyes, corrupt by over-partial looks,
Be anchor'd in the bay where all men ride,
Why of eyes' falsehood hast thou forgëd hooks,
Whereto the judgment of my heart is tied?
Why should my heart think that a several plot
Which my heart knows the wide world's common place?
Or mine eyes seeing this, say this is not,
To put fair truth upon so foul a face?
   In things right true my heart and eyes have erred,
   And to this false plague are they now transferred.

Generated perhaps by the apostrophe to Love as a *fool*, a shower of *f*
sounds falls on the sonnet: *falsehood, forged, fair, foul, face, false*. And, as
Christopher Ricks points out, the *eyes-lies* rhyme in the first quatrain is
pervasive in the sonnets and is of more than metrical significance.[7] The
sonnet is also a treatment of the standard *topos* of the conflict between

---

[7]"Lies," *Critical Inquiry* II (1975): 121–42.

eye and heart, treated explicity in Sonnets 46 and 47. It is interesting, and possibly significant, that the idea of *eyes* being *anchored* has resemblances to other Shakespearean passages dealing with sexual attraction: Cleopatra, boasting of her former sexual conquests, says

> I was
> A morsel for a monarch, and great Pompey
> Would stand and make his eyes grow in my brow;
> There would he anchor his aspect, and die
> With looking on his life.
>
> (I, v, 30–34)

Even the mind's eye, or imagination, which the Elizabethans sometimes called *invention,* could be so anchored, as when Angelo, trying to pray to resist temptation, finds he cannot:

> Heaven hath my empty words,
> Whilst my invention, hearing not my tongue,
> Anchors on Isabel. . . .
>
> (*Measure for Measure*
> II, iv, 2–4)

But we have interrupted the continuity which may exist between Sonnet 141 and the sonnet following. The connecting idea is that of *sin* in line 14 of 141. Sonnet 142 picks it up:

> Love is my sin, and thy dear virtue hate,
> Hate of my sin, grounded on sinful loving:
> O, but with mine compare thou thine own state,
> And thou shalt find it merits not reproving,
> Or if it do, not from those lips of thine,
> That have profan'd their scarlet ornaments,
> And seal'd false bonds of love as oft as mine,
> Robb'd others' beds' revénues of their rents.
> Be it lawful I love thee as thou lov'st those
> Whom thine eyes woo as mine importune thee.
> Root pity in thy heart, that when it grows,
> Thy pity may deserve to pitied be.
>   If thou dost seek to have what thou dost hide,
>   By self-example mayst thou be denied.

Love and hate compound into hateful sin which is grounded upon sinful loving. The Dark Lady's red lips are the sealing wax which have sealed false bonds, and this leads on to the characteristically Shake-spearean figure of "Robb'd others' beds' revénues of their rents," and a consequent appeal to something lawful as contrasted with what went before. But even sin, hate, and guilt may be transformed into some-thing else by a gardening metaphor: "Root pity in thy heart, that when it grows, / Thy pity may deserve to pitied be." Other emotions than pity are said to be *rooted* in Shakespeare: love *(All's Well* IV, v, 12), sorrow *(Macbeth* V, iii, 41), grief and patience *(Cymbeline* IV, ii, 57). Pity is appropriate for a sexual fault, as Othello says so poig-nantly: "But yet the pity of it, Iago! O Iago, the pity of it, Iago!" (IV, i, 195–96).

Readers who visualize the Dark Lady as if she were something like Doll Tearsheet create a false picture, I think. (Some, like John Dover Wilson and Philip Edwards, refer to her as the Dark Woman.) Tucker Brooke, who believed she was as real, and as singular, as Sidney's Stella, has a more accurate picture of her: "She was a harlot, but also a woman of quality; in social rank very likely—for she played the spinet and had a taste, it seems, for courtly verse—and certainly in personality."[8]

The real subject is not the Dark Lady, but the poet's uncontrollable feelings about her. He analyzes them in an allegorical way in Sonnet 147:

> My love is as a fever, longing still
> For that which longer nurseth the disease,
> Feeding on that which doth preserve the ill,
> Th' uncertain sickly appetite to please.
> My reason, the physician to my love,
> Angry that his prescriptions are not kept,
> Hath left me, and I desperate now approve
> Desire is death, which physic did except.
> Past cure I am, now reason is past care,
> And frantic mad with evermore unrest;
> My thoughts and my discourse as madmen's are,
> At randon from the truth vainly express'd;
> > For I have sworn thee fair, and thought thee bright,
> > Who art as black as hell, as dark as night.

---

[8]*Shakespeare's Sonnets* (1936), p. 75.

Those critics who think that such a sonnet could not possibly have been delivered to the Dark Lady should ask themselves if the couplet would be improved if it read

> For I have sworn her fair, and thought her bright,
> Who is as black as hell, as dark as night.

If one accepts the conceit that the speaker's love is a fever and that Reason is the angry physician, the poem is clear enough through line 6. *Approve* means "demonstrate," and line 8 means that Desire, which refused medical treatment from Reason, is fatally ill. Line 9 reverses the proverb "Past cure, past care," but it essentially repeats the meaning of the previous line. The lover is also troubled by the breaking of vows and oaths. These are the compacts of a stable world, whereas the dark, sexual world of the Dark Lady sonnets is one of disorder.

As we observed at the outset, in the sonnets to the Fair Friend it is Time, with its million'd accidents, that creeps in between vows and their fulfillment, but in the sonnets to or about the Dark Lady it is something else. On this theme there are several commentaries, of which Sonnet 152 is one:

> In loving thee thou know'st I am forsworn,
> But thou art twice forsworn, to me love swearing;
> In act thy bed-vow broke, and new faith torn
> In vowing new hate after new love bearing.
> But why of two oaths' breach do I accuse thee,
> When I break twenty? I am perjur'd most,
> For all my vows are oaths but to misuse thee,
> And all my honest faith in thee is lost;
> For I have sworn deep oaths of thy deep kindness,
> Oaths of thy love, thy truth, thy constancy,
> And to enlighten thee gave eyes to blindness,
> Or made them swear against the thing they see;
>> For I have sworn thee fair: more perjur'd eye,
>> To swear against the truth so foul a lie![9]

Here is much ado about swearing oaths and being forsworn (twice or twenty times); it is reminiscent of *Love's Labor's Lost,* where that is a major theme. Vows are made and vows are broken; new faith is torn and honest faith lost. Here *faith* is not the religious term but is

---

[9]Some editors emend *eye* to *I,* obscuring the pun.

equivalent to a vow of love, as in *The Merchant of Venice,* when Portia says to Gratiano, about the ring he has given away, "A thing stuck on with oaths upon your finger, And so riveted with faith unto your flesh" (V, i, 168–69). Line 11 means something like "To illuminate you I claimed that what was invisible was visible." One must recall that the Elizabethans thought that light comes out of the eye instead of into it. The final line combines the theme-word *swear* with the contrasting nouns *truth* and *lie.*

This last word is of course richly ambiguous and provides the thematic material for Sonnet 138:

> When my love swears that she is made of truth,
> I do believe her, though I know she lies,
> That she might think me some untutor'd youth,
> Unlearnèd in the world's false subtleties.
> Thus vainly thinking that she thinks me young,
> Although she knows my days are past the best,
> Simply I credit her false-speaking tongue;
> On both sides thus is simple truth suppress'd.
> But wherefore says she not she is unjust?
> And wherefore say not I that I am old?
> O, love's best habit is in seeming trust,
> And age in love loves not t'have years told.
>   Therefore I lie with her, and she with me,
>   And in our faults by lies we flattered be.

It is of course only in the language of clowns that the simple pun *lies* = "lives" or "dwells" and *lies* = "tells an untruth" exhausts the meaning. Christopher Ricks provides comment on the ubiquity and complexity of the words *lie, lies* (which rhymes with *eyes*), and *lying* (which rhymes with *dying*) in Shakespeare: "The importance of the lie/lie pun is that it concentrates the extraordinarily ranging and profound network of truth-testing situations and postures: it brings mendacity up against those situations and postures which constitute the great moments of endurances of truth: the childbed, the love bed, the bed of sleep and dreams, the sickbed, the deathbed, the grave."[10]

As is the case throughout the sonnets, it is possible to over interpret. Douglas Hamer has given a disciplined interpretation of the couplet:

---

[10]*Op. cit.,* p. 131.

The sonnet tells how Shakespeare and the woman made a love-game of telling white lies about themseves in the hope of making themselves more acceptable: Beatrice and Benedick "lie with" each other in much the same way. Though now always taken in its crude sexual sense, the phrase has only two primary meanings: (a) "Therefore I tell her lies and she me," and (b) "Therefore I fence with her and she with me" (likewise). The sexual sense is accidental, not primary, and is best seen as an associated sexual quibble of the kind so loved by Shakespeare. In sense (b) he uses an image derived from fencing, one ignored by O. E. D. and Onions, but not by Schmidt: "Thou knowest my old ward [guard in fencing]. Here I lay, and thus I bore my point!" (*I Henry IV*, II, iv, 194–95), where "Here I lay" means that he assumed the posture of self-defence, which implies counter-attacking, which posture he illustrates; (ii) "One knows not at what ward you lie!" (*Troilus* I, ii, 259, and "at all these wards I lie" (263), but here, because the topic is Cressida's behaviour, the punning is sleazily sexual, though primary reference is to the posture of self-defence in fencing. The two lines in the sonnet thus mean, "Therefore I fence with her in lies, and she with me, and by lying about our own shortcomings we present ourselves as better than we are." Beds, in short, are out.[11]

I do not think it is possible to exclude totally the sexual implications of "lie with," but I agree with Hamer about the priorities.

Sonnet 138 is one of the two which had appeared in print before the 1609 publication of the whole collection. This was in William Jaggard's curious little miscellany, *The Passionate Pilgrim*, published in 1599 or earlier.[12] The couplet in this version is quite different:

> Therefore I'll lie with love, and love with me,
> Since that our faults in love thus smother'd be.

I think this is clearly a memorial reconstruction and that it is absurd to suppose that this is an early draft which Shakespeare later revised. There is a jocular tone to Sonnet 138; it considers the comical side of amorous entanglements, an aspect which Shakespeare was well aware of when he wrote not only the romantic comedies but also *Romeo and Juliet.*

---

[11]*RES*, n.s. 25 (1974):78.

[12]The first edition survives in only one fragmentary copy, which lacks the title-page, so its date is uncertain. The second edition, which was set up from it, is dated 1599.

Sometimes the playfulness extends to the explicit physical details of sexuality, as in Sonnet 151:

> Love is too young to know what conscience is,
> Yet who knows not conscience is born of love?
> Then, gentle cheater, urge not my amiss,
> Lest guilty of my faults thy sweet self prove:
> For thou betraying me, I do betray
> My nobler part to my gross body's treason;
> My soul doth tell my body that he may
> Triumph in love; flesh stays no farther reason,
> But rising at thy name doth point out thee
> As his triumphant prize. Proud of this pride,
> He is contented thy poor drudge to be,
> To stand in thy affairs, fall by thy side.
> > No want of conscience hold it that I call
> > Her "love" for whose dear love I rise and fall.

The sonnet not only has its comic effects; it is self-consciously comic. Conscience has several meanings: (1) internal moral judgment (2) "consciousness" (3) "of conscience" = "truly." I take "gentle cheater" to be conscience (1); "my nobler part" is of course the soul. It is treason for the body to assume primacy over the soul, but when it does so the soul abdicates (7–8). As often in comic passages, Shakespeare is glancing at a proverb; here it is *Penis erectus conscientiam non habet.* The erection is associated with two meanings of the word *pride,* (1) heightened self-esteem and (2) the height of lust, as in *Lucrece:*

> While Lust is in his pride, no exclamation
> Can curb his heat, or rein his rash desire.
>
> ....
>
> The flesh being proud, Desire doth fight with Grace.

> > > > > (lines 705–6, 712)

Another passage in *Lucrece* illustrates the meaning of the word *will* in several sonnets. Tarquin is replying to Lucrece's pleas not to commit the rape:

> "Thus I forestall thee, if thou mean to chide,
> Thy beauty hath ensnar'd thee to this night,
> Where thou with patience must my will abide—
> My will that marks thee for my earth's delight,

THE TENSION OF THE LYRE

> Which I to conquer sought with all my might;
>   But as reproof and reason beat it dead,
>   By thy bright beauty was it newly bred.
>
> "I see what crosses my attempt will bring,
> I know what thorns the growing rose defends,
> I think the honey guarded with a sting:
> All this beforehand counsel comprehends.
> But Will is deaf and hears no heedful friends. . . .

(lines 484–95)

There is also a proverb "A woman will have her will," which presumably lies behind the first line of Sonnet 135:

> Whoever hath her wish, thou hast thy *Will*,
> And *Will* to boot, and *Will* in overplus;
> More than enough am I that vex thee still,
> To thy sweet will making addition thus,
> Wilt thou, whose will is large and spacious,
> Not once vouchsafe to hide my will in thine?
> Shall will in others seem right gracious,
> And in my will no fair acceptance shine?
> The sea, all water, yet receives rain still,
> And in abundance addeth to his store,
> So thou being rich in *Will* add to thy *Will*
> One will of mine to make thy large *Will* more.
>   Let no unkind, no fair beseechers kill;
>   Think all but one, and me in that one *Will*.

The sonnet is awash with puns, especially on the word *will*. It means at least (1) wish, (2) carnal desire, (3) the sexual organs, both male and female, and (4) the poet himself. This last meaning is made clear by the couplet of the following sonnet, 136:

> Make but my name thy love, and love that still,
> And then thou lovest me, for my name is *Will*.

This brings us very close to the conclusion that the speaker in the Dark Lady sonnets is a man named Will, and that we are to take that person as William Shakespeare. There is evidence from a contemporary that he was known as Will; Thomas Heywood wrote in *The Hierarchie of the Blessed Angels* (1635):

Our moderne Poets to that passe are driuen,
Those names are curtal'd which they first had giuen;
And, as we wisht to haue their memories drown'd,
We scarcely can afford them halfe their sound . . . .
Mellifluous *Shake-speare,* whose inchanting quill
Commanded Mirth or Passion, was but *Will.*[13]

If these sonnets show a certain detachment from the infatuation itself, enough detachment to make games about the sexual relationship,
there is another sonnet which exhibits equal detachment about the
whole Petrarchan tradition to which the love sonnets belong. It at-
tacks, as Du Bellay and Sidney had done, the sonneteers whose poems
are full of the clichés of the type, some of which are listed here:

My mistress' eyes are nothing like the sun,
Coral is far more red than her lips' red;
If snow be white, why then her breasts are dun;
If hairs be wires, black wires grow on her head.
I have seen roses damask'd, red and white,
But no such roses see I in her cheeks,
And in some perfumes is there more delight
Than in the breath that from my mistress reeks.
I love to hear her speak, yet well I know
That music hath a far more pleasing sound:
I grant I never saw a goddess go,
My mistress when she walks treads on the ground.
    And yet, by heaven, I think my love as rare
    As any she belied with false compare.

(130)

This is a clear instance of a sonnet not addressed to the lady herself,
but presumably to the courtly public which was jaded with the sonnets of "Pindare's Apes, flaunt they in phrases fine."[14] It is a companion piece to Sonnet 21, which begins

So it is not with me as with that Muse,
Stirr'd by a painted beauty to his verse,
Who heaven itself for ornament doth use,
And every fair with his fair doth rehearse. . . .

---

[13]E. K. Chambers, *William Shakespeare: A Study of Facts and Problems* (1930), 2:
218–19.
[14]Sidney, *Astrophil and Stella* 3, and for a more particular satiric attack, no. 6.

What these two sonnets show, I think, is that Shakespeare was quite conscious of the poems as public, or semipublic documents, not mere rhapsodies addressed to himself. It does not seem to me that one can draw any serious conclusions about Shakespeare's theories of style from these sonnets. They are conventional, appropriate to his stance as a lover, and not so evidently *jeux d'esprit* as the gulling sonnets of Sir John Davies.[15]

Most readers find a marked contrast between the sonnets to the Fair Friend (or about the Fair Friend) and the sonnets to or about the Dark Lady. There is not much jocularity in the sonnets to the Fair Friend (aside from Sonnet 20, "A woman's face with Nature's own hand painted"), and there is a pervasive beauty in them; they are poems of love. The sonnets to or about the Dark Lady are sometimes adulatory, sometimes analytical, sometimes frivolous; they reflect submission, evasion, and sometimes disgust; they are poems of lust. The most famous of them, 129, is a kind of definition or analysis of lust:

> Th'expense of spirit in a waste of shame
> Is lust in action, and till action, lust
> Is perjur'd, murd'rous, bloody, full of blame,
> Savage, extreme, rude, cruel, not to trust,
> Enjoy'd no sooner but despisëd straight,
> Past reason hunted, and no sooner had,
> Past reason hated as a swallowed bait
> On purpose laid to make the taker mad:
> [Mad] in pursuit and in possession so,
> Had, having, and in quest to have, extreme,
> A bliss in proof, and prov'd, [a] very woe,
> Before, a joy propos'd, behind, a dream.
>   All this the world well knows, yet none knows well
>   To shun the heaven that leads men to this hell.[16]

---

[15]Davies speaks, in his dedicatory sonnet to Sir Anthony Cooke, of

> The bastard Sonnetts of these Rymers bace,
> Which in this whiskinge age are daily borne
> To theire owne shames, and Poetries disgrace.

Poems of Sir John Davies, ed. Robert Krueger (1975), p. 163.

[16]The commentary on this sonnet has a sad history. It includes a chapter in Laura Riding and Robert Graves, *A Survey of Modernist Poetry* (1927), which has been reprinted many times since. Riding and Graves were attempting to justify subtleties of punctuation in the poetry of e e cummings by defending the punctuation of this sonnet in the 1609 edition, which they thought was authorial. Their contentions, in

This is a highly rhetorical sonnet, as many of them are. Carol Thomas Neely has usefully listed rhetorical devices perceptible in it:

This sonnet uses *antimetabole* or *regression,* which turns the sentence around on itself in lines 2 and 14; *anadiplosis,* the repetition of a word at the end of one sentence and the beginning of another, in "mad . . . Mad"; *anaphora,* the repetition of words at the beginning of clauses, in "Past reason hunted . . . Past reason hated"; *polyptoron* or *traductio,* the repetition of words derived from a single root, in "had, having," "proof . . . proov'd"; repeated modifiers in lines 3 and 4; *progression,* or contrary sentences, in "Before, a joy propos'd, behind, a dream," and an additional uncataloguable repetition of the had/mad rhyme at the end and beginning of lines.[17]

Sonnet 129 is of course a meditative rather than a dramatic sonnet; it is certainly not addressed to the Dark Lady, though it is presumably connected with her. It is fairly close to Sonnet 147 ("My love is as a fever, longing still") in content, and that sonnet *is* addressed to the Dark Lady. Psychologically, and with respect to imagery, too, it has a certain relationship with Claudio's comments on lust in *Measure for Measure:*

> As surfeit is the father of much fast,
> So every scope by the immoderate use
> Turns to restraint. Our natures do pursue,
> Like rats that ravin down their proper bane,
> A thirsty evil, and when we drink we die.

(I, ii, 126–30)

"This hell," the conclusion of Sonnet 129, summarizes the qualities of lust, associated with the Dark Lady. As an inhabitant of hell, she

---

so far as they apply to Shakespeare, have been rendered nonsense by a study of the compositors of the 1609 quarto in Eld's printing house by MacD. P. Jackson, "Punctuation and the Compositors of Shakespeare's Sonnets, 1609" *5 Library* 30 (1975): 1–24. Stephen Booth spent several pages in his edition trying to slay the dragon Riding and Graves introduced, but he was not armed with Jackson's sword. Theodore Redpath's essay "The Punctuation of Shakespeare's Sonnets" in Hilton Landry, ed. *New Essays on Shakespeare's Sonnets* ([1976], pp. 217–51) also suffers from ignorance of Jackson's work.

[17]Carol Thomas Neely, "Detachment and Engagement in Shakespeare's Sonnets: 94, 116, and 129," *PMLA* 92 (1977): 95n20. I find myself baffled by Neely's contention that this sonnet is "no conclusion to the dark lady portion of the sequence, but a paradigmatic introduction to it" (p. 91). If the Dark Lady sonnets constitute a sequence (and I fail to see that they do) then they obviously need to be rearranged, and Neely has not, so far as I know, published her rearrangement.

would of course be an evil spirit, which she is called in the sonnet which should logically introduce the triangular situation. It is the other sonnet published in 1599 in *The Passionate Pilgrim,* and it becomes 144 in the 1609 edition:

> Two loves I have of comfort and despair,
> Which like two spirits do suggest me still:
> The better angel is a man right fair,
> The worser spirit a woman color'd ill.
> To win me soon to hell, my female evil
> Tempteth my better angel from my [side],
> And would corrupt my saint to be a devil,
> Wooing his purity with her foul pride.
> And whether that my angel be turn'd fiend
> Suspect I may, yet not directly tell,
> But being both from me, both to each friend,
> I guess one angel in another's hell.
>> Yet this shall I ne'er know, but live in doubt,
>> Till my bad angel fire my good one out.

The word *comfort* is applied to the Fair Friend in Sonnet 48.6. *Suggest* means "tempt" and *still* means "constantly." *Foul pride* has the same sexual significance as it does in Sonnet 151. *Friend* and *fiend* rhyme in *Venus and Adonis* (638–40) and *fiend* rhymes with *end* in Sonnet 145 and *The Phoenix and Turtle.* The last line completes the conceit of the bad angel in hell but adds a punning allusion to venereal disease, which may be illustrated from a passage in *2 Henry IV* II, iv, 335–40):

Fal. For the boy, there is a good angel about him, but the devil blinds him too.
Prince: For the women?
Fal. For one of them [Doll Tearsheet] she's in hell already, and burns poor souls; for th'other, [Mrs. Quickly] I owe her money, and whether she be damn'd for that, I know not.

If the situation of the Fair Friend being seduced by the Dark Lady is complicated, the feelings of the poet are even more complicated. He persists in keeping the moral distinction between the two alive, but he is capable of some very elaborate juggling to justify his attitudes. Here we must return to three sonnets addressed to the Fair Friend, numbers 40–42. In Sonnet 40 his paradoxical attitude is displayed:

I do forgive thy robb'ry, gentle thief,
Although thou steal thee all my poverty;
And yet love knows it is a greater grief
To bear love's wrong than hate's known injury.
    Lascivious grace, in whom all ill well shows,
    Kill me with spites, yet we must not be foes.

                            (40.9–14)

Sometimes the triangle seems merely an occasion for the exercise of wit and ingenuity. The poet excuses the Fair Friend's lasciviousness because of his youth and beauty, and because the invitation came from the lady: who would be so ungallant as to turn her down?

Ay me, but yet thou mightst my seat forbear,
And chide thy beauty and thy straying youth,
Who lead thee in their riot even there
Where thou art forc'd to break a twofold truth:
    Hers by thy beauty tempting her to thee,
    Thine by thy beauty being false to me.

                            (41.9–14)

My seat is to be understood in the same sense it bears in *Othello* when Iago in soliloquy gives some of his reasons for wanting revenge on Othello:

But partly led to diet my revenge,
For that I do suppose the lusty Moor
Hath leap'd into my seat . . .

                         (II, i, 294–96)

Riot does not have its modern meaning; rather, it signifies unbridled sensuality and dissipation, as when the dying John of Gaunt says of Richard II:

His rash fierce blaze of riot cannot last,
For violent fires soon burn out themselves.

                         (II, i, 33–34)

In the last of the three misplaced sonnets, 42, the poet casuistically works up to the conclusion

But here's the joy, my friend and I are one;
Sweet flattery! then she loves but me alone.

But before that he has attempted to find excuses for the friend and his mistress:

That thou hast her, it is not all my grief,
And yet it may be said I lov'd her dearly;
That she hath thee is of my wailing chief,
A loss in love that touches me more nearly.
Loving offenders, thus I will excuse ye:
Thou dost love her because thou know'st I love her,
And for my sake even so doth she abuse me,
Suff'ring my friend for my sake to approve her.

This passage is illuminated by the comment of M. M. Mahood:

The dramatic irony of the plays, where the audience knows the character to be wide of the mark, is matched in the sonnet by the irony with which Shakespeare contemplates himself excusing the inexcusable, and which is conveyed by the wordplay upon *excuse* and *approve*. Excuse, besides meaning "make excuses, even where there is no justification for them" has the ironically impossible meaning of "exculpate"; while if the youth approves the woman in the sexual sense, he can scarcely approve of her in the moral one. The incompatibility of these two sets of meanings explains as well as conveys Shakespeare's serene and witty detachment from the whole affair.[18]

Sonnets 139 and 140 deal with this question of finding excuses. The former says

Let me excuse thee: ah, my love well knows
Her pretty looks have been mine enemies,
And therefore from my face she turns my foes,
That they elsewhere might dart their injuries:

(139.9–12)

Some editors believe that everything following the colon after *thee* is direct speech and should so be punctuated. The puzzle, however, is not the mode of discourse but in the tricky identification of *enemies* and *foes*. The *pretty* (i.e., wanton) looks have been the speaker's enemies, but when she turns them away from his face it is as if she is directing them elsewhere, but she is still doing injury with them, this time to the Fair Friend.

In Sonnet 140 there is a reference to the surrounding world, and its condition is seen as having something to do with the tangled love portrayed here:

---

[18]*Shakespeare's Wordplay* (1957), pp. 90–91.

If I might teach thee wit, better it were,
Though not to love, yet, love, to tell me so,
As testy sick men, when their deaths be near,
No news but health from their physicians know,
For if I should despair, I should go mad,
And in my madness might speak ill of thee;
Now this ill-wresting world is grown so bad,
Mad slanderers by mad ears believèd be.

(140.5–12)

Sonnets 133 and 134 deal with the conceit that the triangle produces a curious kind of imprisonment:

Prison my heart in thy steel bosom's ward,
But then my friend's heart let my poor heart bail;
Whoe'er keeps me, let my heart be his guard,
Thou canst not then use rigor in my jail:
    And yet thou wilt, for I being pent in thee,
    Perforce am thine, and all that is in me.

(133.9–14)

The couplet of 134 may sum up the whole situation:

Him have I lost, thou hast both him and me,
He pays the whole, and yet am I not free.

Of all the themes in the sonnets, the one pursued most intently by Shakespeare is the notion of appearance, "show," outward beauty, as contrasted with worth, "truth," virtue. Raymond Southall has a good description of it: "As in writing about his poetry Shakespeare distinguishes between manner and matter, so in general he distinguishes in the sonnets between appearances (likened after the idiom of the time to raiment, painting, and ornament) and inward worth. . . . The attitude which eventually prevails in the sonnets is . . . grounded in the perception that the measure of true worth is 'within.' It is not sufficient that, in the words of Sonnet 53, 'In all external grace you have some part,' for

How like Eve's apple doth thy beauty grow
If thy sweet virtue answer not thy show."[19]

---

[19]*Literature and the Rise of Capitalism* (1973), pp. 47–48.

It is in this context, I think, that the famous and much discussed "Christian" sonnet, 146, should be read:

> Poor soul, the centre of my sinful earth,
> [. . . .] these rebel pow'rs that thee array,
> Why dost thou pine within and suffer dearth,
> Painting thy outward walls so costly gay?
> Why so large cost, having so short a lease,
> Dost thou upon thy fading mansion spend?
> Shall worms, inheritors of this excess,
> Eat up thy charge? Is this thy body's end?
> Then, soul, live thou upon thy servant's loss,
> And let that pine to aggravate thy store;
> Buy terms divine in selling hours of dross;
> Within be fed, without be rich no more:
> So shalt thou feed on Death, that feeds on men,
> And Death once dead, there's no more dying then.[20]

Unfortunately there are some textual problems in this sonnet in addition to the critical ones. At the beginning of the second line the compositor carelessly repeated the last three words of line 1. (This fault, called dittography, is not uncommon, in handwriting and typing as well as printing.) What words or syllables should be substituted is an open, or almost open, question. Ingram and Redpath compiled a list of 400 words used by Shakespeare "which seemed to make any kind of sense and fitted the metrical pattern." They then discarded 300 of these, for one reason or another, and listed the remaining 100 in an appendix to their edition. Half of these they looked on favorably. "In our view it is from these fifty readings that any editor of the Sonnets

---

[20]The critical comment on this sonnet is overwhelming. Booth devotes some sixteen pages to it. Giorgio Melchiori has a chapter called "Sonnet 146 and the Ethics of Religion" in his *Shakespeare's Dramatic Meditations* (1976). A local skirmish between B. C. Southam, "Shakespeare's Christian Sonnet, No. 146," *SQ* 11 (1960): 67–71, and Charles A. Huttar, "The Christian Basis of Shakespeare's Sonnet 146," *SQ* 19 (1968) leaves the main battle indecisive. Albert S. Gérard discussed "Iconic Organization in Shakespeare's Sonnet 146" in *English Studies* 42 (1961): 157–59, and Michael West treats the body-soul debate in "The Internal Dialogue of Shakespeare's Sonnet 146" in *SQ* 25 (1974): 109–22. Several of these refer to an essay by the late Donald A. Stauffer of Princeton called "Critical Principles and a Sonnet" in *American Scholar* 12 (1943): 52–62, but Thomas P. Roche, Jr., currently of Princeton, calls it "pretentious rubbish," *SQ* 29 (1978):444.

wishing to print an emendation would have to choose."[21] One's choice would depend in part upon how he glossed *array* at the end of the line. Elsewhere in Shakespeare *array* as a verb means only "to clothe or dress," but as a noun one of its meanings is "order of troops in march or battle" (Schmidt 2) and it is quite characteristic of Shakespeare to make a verb out of a noun. There are several threads of imagery intertwined in this sonnet: a besieged castle, decorating a mansion ("painting thy outward walls"), starving and eating, renting or leasing for various periods of time, living and dying. The body is indicated in several figures: "my sinful earth," "thy outward walls," "thy fading mansion," and "thy servant."

Another famous Elizabethan poem consists of an address to the soul: Sir Walter Ralegh's "The Lie" begins

> Go, soul, the body's guest,
> Upon a thankless errand;
> Fear not to touch the best;
> The truth shall be thy warrant.
> Go, since I needs must die,
> And give the world the lie.

Ralegh's poem is of course a satire, which Shakespeare's is not. In fact, it is more like a sermon. The four rhetorical questions in rapid sequence in the first eight lines subside into didactic advice in the sestet. The tone changes and attention is focused on paired opposites: *live* and *loss: Let that pine* meaning "let the body starve or dwindle," as the soul was doing in line 3 to *aggravate thy store,* "to increase [without any unfavorable connotation] the soul's plentiful resources." The debate of the soul and the body is an ancient *topos*. Ordinarily this sonnet is considered to embody Christian doctrine: *my sinful earth* is not consistent with the claim some make that the poem is Platonic, not Christian. The final couplet, which troubles some readers, is not very far from the concluding couplet of one of Donne's Holy Sonnets:

> One short sleep past, we wake eternally,
> And death shall be no more, Death thou shalt die.[22]

---

[21]*Shakespeare's Sonnets,* ed. W. G. Ingram and Theodore Redpath (1965), pp. 336–38 and 358–59.
[22]Holy Sonnet X, "Death, be not proud."

The association of death with eating is characteristically Shakespear-ean; it appears in the couplet of the first sonnet in the 1609 collection:

> Pity the world, or else this glutton be
> To eat the world's due, by the grave and thee.

The simplest meaning of "the world's due" is that given by Malone, the propagation of the species, in which *the world* seems al-most equivalent to Nature. That there was an obligation to supply offspring is generally recognized in Shakespeare. It is expressed com-ically by Benedick when he is converted into a lover: "Shall quips and sentences and these paper bullets of the brain awe a man from the career of his humor? No, the world must be peopled. When I said I would die a bachelor, I did not think I should live till I were married" (*Much Ado* II, iii, 240–43). Very often in Shakespeare, particularly in the sonnets, *the world* is not external nature but society, or more specifically, what society thinks or believes. *The world* could, of course, in that pre-Space age, mean the universe, but it could also mean the microcosm. Sometimes it is another consciousness, as in the first lines of Sonnet 107:

> Not mine own fears, nor the prophetic soul
> Of the wide world, dreaming on things to come. . . .

Though the world contains great beauty, it also contains great evil, and for those who inhabit it, that evil is unescapable.

CHAPTER FOUR

Dramatic Poems and Poetic Plays

It would not be surprising to find that Shakespeare's nondramatic poems, particularly *Venus and Adonis* and *Lucrece,* have traits in common with the sonnets.[1] All these poems were written without the constraints of the stage or the technical necessities of the actors to shape them. Many attempts to fix a date for the sonnets conclude that some of them suit the period 1592–94, when the two narrative poems were written and published.

There are, however, significant differences which should not be overlooked. The two long poems were based upon well-known classical material, Ovid in the case of *Venus and Adonis,* Ovid and Livy in the case of *Lucrece.* They were addressed to a courtly audience and were dedicated, in prefaces by the author, to the earl of Southampton. They were printed by a fellow Stratfordian, Richard Field. No such clarity surrounds the sonnets. How they got into print is a tantalizing mystery. To whom they are addressed is unknown. The audience or audiences addressed in the sonnets can only be guessed from the poems themselves. Furthermore they were not, like the classical narratives, published when the genre to which they belong was at the height of fashion.

The most obvious similarity between *Venus and Adonis* and the sonnets is in that passage in which Venus argues with the reluctant Adonis that he has a duty to hand on his beauty to future generations.

> "Torches are made to light, jewels to wear,
> Dainties to taste, fresh beauty for the use,

---

[1] *A Lover's Complaint* and *The Phoenix and Turtle* are less obviously connected to the sonnets, although *A Lover's Complaint* was published with them. This may have been merely a publisher's notion of convention: Daniel's *Complaint of Rosamund* was published with his sonnet cycle *Delia* in 1592.

Herbs for their smell, and sappy plants to bear:
Things growing to themselves are growth's abuse.
   Seeds spring from seeds, and beauty breedeth beauty;
   Thou wast begot, to get it is thy duty.

"Upon the earth's increase why shouldst thou feed,
Unless the earth with thy increase be fed?
By law of nature thou art bound to breed,
That thine may live, when thou thyself art dead;
   And so in spite of death thou dost survive,
   In that thy likeness still is left alive."

(163–74)

Venus' argument is of course the general theme of Sonnets 1–17, but the circumstances are completely different. In one case the amorous goddess is trying to seduce a shy and reluctant youth more interested in hunting than in love; in the other an older poet is trying to persuade a younger man to marry and have children. I see no way of telling with certainty which treatment came first. But it is worth noting that the stanza form of *Venus and Adonis* is a quatrain and a couplet, like the sestet of a sonnet.

Adonis' comparison of love and lust has some resemblance to the sonnets on lust, particularly 129 ("Th' expense of spirit in a waste of shame") and 147 ("My love is as a fever, longing still"):

"Call it not love, for Love to heaven is fled,
Since sweating Lust on earth usurp'd his name,
Under whose simple semblance he hath fed
Upon fresh beauty, blotting it with blame;
   Which the hot tyrant stains, and soon bereaves,
   As caterpillars do the tender leaves.

"Love comforteth like sunshine after rain,
But Lust's effect is tempest after sun;
Love's gentle spring doth always fresh remain,
Lust's winter comes ere summer half be done;
   Love surfeits not, Lust like a glutton dies;
   Love is all truth, Lust full of forgèd lies."

(793–804)

In both *Venus and Adonis* and Sonnet 56 separation from a loved one is compared to separation by an ocean:

> Which after him she darts, as one on shore
> Gazing upon a late embarkèd friend,
> Till the wild waves will have him seen no more,
> Whose ridges with the meeting clouds contend . . .
>
> (817–20)

and

> Let this sad int'rim like the ocean be
> Which parts the shore, where two contracted new
> Come daily to the banks, that when they see
> Return of love, more blest may be the view. . . .
>
> (56.9–12)

Many lines, phrases, and words in *Venus and Adonis* prefigure or recall similar passages in the sonnets: "Look in mine eyeballs, there thy beauty lies" (119); "Give me one kiss, I'll give it thee again, / And one for int'rest, if thou wilt have twain" (209–10); "'In night' quoth she 'desire sees best of all'" (720); "For he being dead, with him is beauty slain, / And beauty dead, black chaos comes again" (1,019–20); "Alas, poor world, what treasure hast thou lost!" (1,075). Such reverberations are often of familiar sentiments or commonplace expressions, but they can illustrate to the reader of the sonnets how much Shakespeare's language in them is a distillation of the language he uses elsewhere.

Lucrece belongs to a different genre from *Venus and Adonis*. It is a complaint poem. This genre, popular in the 1590s, presented the ghost of a famous woman complaining of her sad fate. Samuel Daniel had appended to his sonnet cycle *Delia* in 1592 *The Complaint of Rosamund*, about the fair mistress of Henry II who was poisoned by his queen, Eleanor of Aquitaine. Shakespeare knew Daniel's poem and to some extent followed it (in verse form, for example) but he did not make his heroine a ghost, presumably to make the poem more dramatic. Not only is *Lucrece* the "graver labor" which Shakespeare promised to his patron, the earl of Southampton, in the dedication to *Venus and Adonis;* it is more obviously the work of a playwright.[2]

---

[2]I discuss the place of *Lucrece* in its genre in *Elizabethan Poetry* (1952) pp. 111–16. Gabriel Harvey's comment is "The younger sort takes much delight in *Venus and Adonis*, but his *Lucrece*, and his tragedy of *Hamlet, Prince of Denmark*, have it in them to please the wiser sort" (*Gabriel Harvey's Marginalia*, ed. G. C. Moore Smith [1913] p. 232). *Lucrece* is the title on the title page of the 1594 quarto; *The Rape of Lucrece* is the title on the first page of text and the running title throughout.

Like its predecessor, *Lucrece* has some connection with the sonnets. The most obvious is the passage on lust at the climax of the poem:

> But she hath lost a dearer thing than life,
> And he hath won what he would lose again;
> This forcëd league doth force a further strife,
> This momentary joy breeds months of pain,
> This hot desire converts to cold disdain;
> > Pure Chastity is rifled of her store,
> > And Lust, the thief, far poorer than before.
>
> Look as the full-fed hound or gorgëd hawk,
> Unapt for tender smell, or speedy flight,
> Make slow pursuit, or altogether balk
> The prey wherein by nature they delight,
> So surfeit-taking Tarquin fares this night:
> > His taste delicious, in digestion souring.
> > Devours his will, that liv'd by foul devouring.
>
> O, deeper sin than bottomless conceit
> Can comprehend in still imagination!
> Drunken Desire must vomit his receipt
> Ere he can see his own abomination.
> While Lust is in his pride, no exclamation
> > Can curb his heat, or rein his rash desire,
> > Till like a jade, Self-will himself doth tire.

(687–707)

The relationship with Sonnet 129 ("Th' expense of spirit in a waste of shame") is easy to see. The conflict between reason and will, a theme in the sonnets, also appears in Tarquin's soliloquy:

> "I'll beg her love: but she is not her own;
> The worst is but denial and reproving.
> My will is strong, past reason's weak removing:
> > Who fears a sentence or an old man's saw
> > Shall by a painted cloth be kept in awe."

(241–45)

Many further phrases and images are like those in the sonnets: the sun obscured by clouds (373 and 777); conflict between eye and heart (276); summer as perfection (837); fountains and mud (850); the body the mansion of the soul (1,170–71); and perhaps most vividly, the portrait of Hecuba as "Time's ruin, beauty's wrack" (1,451).

I have maintained, in an essay on the influence of Shakespeare's non-dramatic poems,[3] that, granting the popularity of Shakespeare's poems in his lifetime and the several imitations of them, the greatest and most significant influence of *Venus and Adonis* and *Lucrece* was upon Shakespeare's own later work. Though it cannot be demonstrated clearly that the sonnets, or most of them, are later than the narrative poems, I think that they probably are, and that the richness of those two dated narrative poems contributes to the timeless beauty of the sonnets.

II

Three notable sonnets, 97, 98, and 99, develop the idea that absence can be related to the seasons, that love is expressed in imagery of nature—that winter, spring and their characteristic flora are the objective correlative of a lover's feelings. Sonnet 97 is very different from those predominantly moral sonnets that precede it in the 1609 order:

> How like a winter hath my absence been
> From thee, the pleasure of the fleeting year!
> What freezings have I felt, what dark days seen!
> What old December's bareness every where!
> And yet this time remov'd was summer's time,
> The teeming autumn, big with rich increase,
> Bearing the wanton burthen of the prime,
> Like widowed wombs after their lords' decease:
> Yet this abundant issue seem'd to me
> But hope of orphans and unfathered fruit,
> For summer and his pleasures wait on thee,
> And thou away, the very birds are mute;
>   Or if they sing, 'tis with so dull a cheer
>   That leaves look pale, dreading the winter's near.

The Fair Friend is "the pleasure of the fleeting year," yet absence from him has been the hardest part of that year. In a song in *As You Like It,* winter and rough weather are described as the only enemy of man in a

---

[3] "The Non-Dramatic Poems" in *Shakespeare: Aspects of Influence,* ed. G.B. Evans, *Harvard English Studies* 7 (1976): 43–53.

pastoral environment, and here the hardships are freezing tempera-
tures, dark days, and December's bareness. The alliteration and the
compact catalog give this description a powerful effect. The second
quatrain declares that the previous description was metaphorical, that
the time of absence was summer or autumn, with nature producing its
offspring after the father, spring, had expired. But the speaker finds no
joy in the "abundant issue," for "summer and his pleasures" stay with
the Friend, and in absence the speaker finds nature unresponsive; fear-
ing winter, the birds and the leaves symbolize his emotion.

When Proteus and Valentine discuss love at the beginning of *Two
Gentlemen of Verona*, they use similar imagery. Valentine, not yet a victim of love, says

> Even so by love the young and tender wit
> Is turn'd to folly, blasting in the bud,
> Losing his verdure, even in the prime,
> And all the fair affects of future hopes.[4]

(I, i, 47-50)

Sonnet 98 is a variation on the same theme:

> From you I have been absent in the spring,
> When proud-pied April, (dress'd in all his trim)
> Hath put a spirit of youth in every thing,
> That heavy Saturn laugh'd and leapt with him,
> Yet nor the lays of birds, nor the sweet smell
> Of different flowers in odor and in hue,
> Could make me any summer's story tell,
> Or from their proud lap pluck them where they grew;
> Nor did I wonder at the lily's white,
> Nor praise the deep vermilion in the rose,
> They were but sweet, but figures of delight,
> Drawn after you, you pattern of all those.
>   Yet seem'd it winter still, and, you away,
>   As with your shadow I with these did play.

The identification of love with the season of spring is the source of
another, very famous, Shakespearean image in *Two Gentlemen of
Verona*:

---

[4]The identification of seasons and weather with the lover's feeling was of course a
conventional Petrarchan conceit. J. B. Leishman thought Sonnet 97 to be an echo of
Petrarch's famous "Zefiro torna," but Shakespeare shows very little if any direct
borrowing from Petrarch in the sonnets.

> O, how this spring of love resembleth
> The uncertain glory of an April day,
> Which now shows all the beauty of the sun,
> And by and by a cloud takes all away.

(I, iii, 84–87)

When the Duke tricks Valentine into lending him his cloak he finds in it a ten-line sonnet fragment and a note to Silvia that tonight he will rescue her (III, i, 140–49). Valentine's subsequent lament over his banishment (III, i, 170–87) is entirely in the style of the Petrarchan lover.

The language of love is not infinite, though Troilus believes that desire is boundless (*Troilus and Cressida* III, ii, 83); accordingly, it is not surprising that there are similarities between the expression of love in the plays and in the sonnets. In *Two Gentlemen,* however, we find a closer correspondence in the Renaissance theme of the conflict between romantic love and male friendship.

In the final scene of the play, often denounced by the critics, there is a highly theatrical demonstration of this conflict. Silvia is reproaching Proteus for his pursuit of her when he should have been loyal to his first love, Julia, and to his friend Valentine:

> Read over Julia's heart (thy first best love),
> For whose dear sake thou didst then rend thy faith
> Into a thousand oaths; and all those oaths
> Descended into perjury, to love me.
> Thou hast no faith left now, unless thou'dst two,
> And that's far worse than none: better have none
> Than plural faith, which is too much by one.
> Thy counterfeit to thy true friend!

Pro.   In love
> Who respects friend?

Sil.   All men but Proteus.

(V, iv, 46–54)

The theatricality of the scene depends upon the fact that Julia is present, in disguise as a boy, and Valentine is close by, in hiding. When Proteus threatens to force Silvia to yield to his desire, Valentine steps forward and rescues her. Proteus immediately repents and Valentine as promptly forgives him, making the extraordinary (to modern taste) gesture of surrendering to him all claim to Silvia. Such was the extreme exhibition of the ancient code of male friendship. Quiller-Couch was so shocked at this behavior that he concluded that there are *no*

75

gentlemen in Verona.[5] At this point Julia faints, her identity is discovered, things are hastily patched up and every Jack has his Jill.

The triangle in the sonnets is somewhat puzzling to modern readers because what is considered "normal" jealousy seems lacking in the Poet. According to Sonnet 41 the Fair Friend, like Proteus, was doubly disloyal:

> Those pretty wrongs that liberty commits
> When I am sometime absent from thy heart,
> Thy beauty and thy years full well befits,
> For still temptation follows where thou art.
> Gentle thou art, and therefore to be won,
> Beauteous thou art, therefore to be assailed;
> And when a woman woos, what woman's son
> Will sourly leave her till [she] have prevailed?
> Ay me, but yet thou mightst my seat forbear,
> And chide thy beauty and thy straying youth,
> Who lead thee in their riot even there
> Where thou art forc'd to break a twofold truth:
> Hers by thy beauty tempting her to thee,
> Thine by thy beauty being false to me.

"Pretty wrongs" are to be understood in the sense of Pandarus' final remark when he brings Troilus and Cressida together: "I will show you a chamber, which bed, because it shall not speak of your pretty encounters, press it to death" (*Troilus and Cressida* III, ii, 207–09). "Liberty" means not only freedom from restraint but also sexual misconduct, as in *Measure for Measure* when Claudio explains the cause of his arrest for getting Juliet pregnant as "too much liberty" (I, ii, 125). Structurally, the first eight lines excuse the Friend because the Dark Lady, overcome by his beauty, did the seducing; the third quatrain reproaches the Friend nevertheless; the couplet resolves it all with a paradox about beauty. "Riot" in line 11 means "dissoluteness," not "public turmoil," as when the newly crowned and reformed Henry V calls Falstaff "The tutor and the feeder of my riots" (*2 Henry IV* V, v, 62).

The semi-serious or casuistical tone of Sonnet 41 is maintained and perhaps increased in Sonnet 42:

---

[5]New Cambridge Shakespeare *Two Gentlemen of Verona*, (1921), p. xiv.

That thou hast her, it is not all my grief,
And yet it may be said I lov'd her dearly;
That she hath thee is of my wailing chief,
A loss in love that touches me more nearly.
Loving offenders, thus I will excuse ye:
Thou dost love her because thou know'st I love her,
And for my sake even so doth she abuse me,
Suff'ring my friend for my sake to approve her.
If I lose thee, my loss is my love's gain,
And losing her, my friend hath found that loss;
Both find each other, and I lose both twain,
And both for my sake lay on me this cross.
    But here's the joy, my friend and I are one;
    Sweet flattery! then she loves but me alone.

The connection between this sonnet and the plays has been well described by M. M. Mahood:

The tone of these lines suggests, however, that Shakespeare here handles his own experience with exactly that blend of implication and detachment that, as a dramatist, he communicates to his audience, making us, in the plays, both share and survey a character's use of this "mechanism of escape." The situation arises when Lear seeks excuses for the failure of Regan and Cornwall to come and greet him, and when Desdemona, with even greater pathos, struggles to explain away Othello's first outburst of fury. The dramatic irony of the plays, where the audience knows the character to be wide of the mark, is matched in the sonnet by the irony with which Shakespeare contemplates himself excusing the inexcusable, and which is conveyed by the wordplay upon *excuse* and *approve*. *Excuse,* besides meaning "make excuses, even where there is no justification for them" has the ironically impossible meaning of "exculpate"; while if the youth *approves* the woman in the sexual sense, he can scarcely approve of her in the moral one. The incompatibility of these two sets of meanings explains as well as conveys Shakespeare's serene and witty detachment from the whole affair. The play on *excuse* shows that the youth's rivalry with Shakespeare's mistress troubles the poet far less than the sins of the spirit which he reproaches in more troubled sonnets, and the *approve* pun reflects Shakespeare's relief, after some anxiety, that the youth's behaviour is mere wild-oat experimentation and that he is not wasting high feeling on a woman whom the poet knows by experience to be little worth it. Shakespeare has understood the situation well enough to show his own role in it as a serio-comic one. No one could believe such

77

fantastic rationalizations as are constructed here; Shakespeare himself mocks them, although he knows the unhappiness that constructs them.[6]

III

Love's Labor's Lost, a comedy about masculine attempts to renounce love in favor of an academy devoted to study and the pursuit of fame, has many links with the sonnets. As Anne Barton points out, "Navarre's image of 'cormorant devouring Time' (I, i, 4) is near-allied to that 'devouring Time' of the sonnets which blunts the lion's paws and burns the long-lived Phoenix in her blood. In the sonnets Shakespeare proposes two weapons against Time: children and, more persuasively, poetry."[7] But there are many other themes: swearing and being forsworn, in IV, ii, 105 and in Sonnet 152:

> In loving thee thou know'st I am forsworn,
> But thou art twice forsworn, to me love swearing. . . .

When Boyet speaks of "the heart's still rhetoric, disclosed with eyes" (II, i, 229) we are reminded of "What strainèd touches rhetoric can lend" (82.10) and

> O me! what eyes hath Love put in my head,
> Which have no correspondence with true sight, . . .
>
> (148.1–2)

Although it is thoroughly conventional, Berowne's request,

> Mistress, look on me,
> Behold the window of my heart, mine eye,
>
> (V, ii, 837–38)

is elaborated in Sonnet 24:

> For through the painter must you see his skill,
> To find where your true image pictur'd lies,
> Which in my bosom's shop is hanging still,
> That hath his windows glazèd with thine eyes.
> Now see what good turns eyes for eyes have done:
> Mine eyes have drawn thy shape, and thine for me
> Are windows to my breast, wherethrough the sun
> Delights to peep, to gaze therein on thee.
>
> (24.5–12)

---

[6]*Shakespeare's Wordplay* (1957), pp. 90–91.
[7]*The Riverside Shakespeare* (1974), p. 175b.

To describe *Love's Labor's Lost* as a comedy about love is to give an incomplete description. It is also a play about language.[8] All kinds of language are exploited, exaggerated, satirized. Courtly wit, bombastic Marlowesque boasting, incorrigible but lovable stupidity, all are played one against another. "Sweet smoke of rhetoric!" exclaims the braggart Spaniard, Don Armado, when his page Moth makes a clever quip. But Berowne, the most intelligent male character in the play, finally forswears rhetoric in a most rhetorical way:

> O, never will I trust to speeches penn'd,
> Nor to the motion of a schoolboy's tongue,
> Nor never come in vizard to my friend,
> Nor woo in rhyme, like a blind harper's song!
> Taffata phrases, silken terms precise,
> Three-piled hyperboles, spruce affection,
> Figures pedantical—these summer flies
> Have blown me full of maggot ostentation.
> I do forswear them, and I here protest,
> By this white glove (how white the hand, God knows!)
> Henceforth my wooing mind shall be express'd
> In russet yeas and honest kersey noes.
>
> (V, ii, 402–13)

In the Rival Poet sonnets Shakespeare also discourses, though often indirectly, on matters of style. He sounds somewhat like Berowne when he says, in Sonnet 82, speaking of other poets

> yet when they have devis'd
> What strainëd touches rhetoric can lend,
> Thou, truly fair, wert truly sympathiz'd
> In true plain words by thy true-telling friend.
>
> (82.9–12)

In Sonnet 76 he also compares his style with that of currently fashionable poets:

> Why is my verse so barren of new pride?
> So far from variation or quick change?
> Why with the time do I not glance aside
> To new-found methods and to compounds strange?

---

[8]See William C. Carroll, *The Great Feast of Languages in* Love's Labor's Lost (1976).

It is of course conventional that the writer of love sonnets pretends that he uses no art, that his hyperbolical declarations are simple truth, without exaggeration. The best known of these protestations is probably Sidney's Sonnet 74 in *Astrophil and Stella*, though it follows the model of several Petrarchan poets, especially DuBellay and Ronsard:

> I never drank of Aganippe well,
> Nor ever did in shade of Tempe sit,
> And Muses scorn with vulgar brains to dwell,
> Poor layman I, for sacred rites unfit . . .

His more specific attack on fashionable sonneteers (though it was largely Sidney who started the sonneteering fashion in England) is in *Astrophil and Stella* 15:

> You that do search for every purling spring
> Which from the ribs of old Parnassus flows,
> And every flower, not sweet perhaps, which grows
> Near thereabout, into your poesy wring;
> You that do dictionary's method bring
> Into your rhymes, running in rattling rows;
> You that poor Petrarch's long-deceasëd woes
> With new-born sighs and denizened wit do sing;
> You take wrong ways,—those far-fet helps be such
> As do bewray a want of inward touch,
> And sure at length stol'n goods do come to light.
> But if, both for your love and skill, your name
> You seek to nurse at fullest breasts of fame,
> Stella behold, and then begin t'endite.

Sidney has other sonnets to the same effect, numbers 1, 3, and 6 in *Astrophil and Stella*. Although he professes to eschew all kinds of tropes, figures and conceits, his editor William Ringler says, "one of the main characteristics distinguishing Sidney's own poetry from the earlier work of his countrymen is its complex rhetorical elaboration."[9]

Shakespeare's own attack upon the clichés of the Petrarchan blazons comes considerably later than Sidney's. By the time it was written the atmosphere of adulation must have been stifling. Shakespeare's tone, however, is not didactic like Sidney's, but is amusingly ironic. He

---

[9] *The Poems of Sir Philip Sidney* (1962), p. 460.

compares his mistress' traits, unfavorably, to those alleged for the Petrarchan mistresses, yet concludes that she is in no way inferior to them:

> My mistress' eyes are nothing like the sun,
> Coral is far more red than her lips' red;
> If snow be white, why then her breasts are dun;
> If hairs be wires, black wires grow on her head.
> I have seen roses damask'd, red and white,
> But no such roses see I in her cheeks,
> And in some perfumes is there more delight
> Than in the breath that from my mistress reeks.
> I love to hear her speak, yet well I know
> That music hath a far more pleasing sound;
> I grant I never saw a goddess go,
> My mistress when she walks treads on the ground.
>   And yet, by heaven, I think my love as rare
>   As any she belied with false compare.
>
> (130)

In a declarative tone, this sonnet first rejects two comparisons ordinarily made by sonneteers in praise of the lady's eyes and lips. Then, when comparisons are admitted, the details become absurd: dun breasts and black wires. The poet inserts himself into the poem after the first quatrain: the first personal singular pronoun occurs seven times in the rest of the sonnet. To counter the extravagance of conventional praise, the speaker is moderate and ironical: "in *some* perfumes is there more delight"—not all, perhaps, but some. He admits that he loves to hear her speak, but insists calmly that music is more pleasing. He concedes that he is no judge of how goddesses walk, but his mistress' feet are on the solid earth. The couplet then shifts, epigrammatically, to praise her as "rare" (admirable, extraordinary, as in the epitaph O RARE BEN JOHNSON in Westminster Abbey, or the remark Agrippa makes when he hears Enobarbus' description of Cleopatra in her barge on the river Cydnus: "O rare for Antony!") as any "she" misrepresented by false comparisons.

It has often been suggested that there may be a connection between the Dark Lady, the "woman color'd ill" of Sonnet 144 and Rosaline in *Love's Labor's Lost*. We get a description of Rosaline from Berowne in his Henry Higgins mood, just after discovering in himself a regrettable tendency to fall in love:

81

What! I love, I sue, I seek a wife—
A woman, that is like a German [clock],
Still a-repairing, ever out of frame,
And never going aright, being a watch,
But being watch'd that it may still go right!
Nay, to be perjur'd, which is worst of all;
And among three to love the worst of all,
A whitely wanton with a velvet brow,
With two pitch-balls stuck in her face for eyes;
Ay, and by heaven, one that will do the deed
Though Argus were her eunuch and her guard.
And I to sigh for her, to watch for her,
To pray for her, go to! It is a plague
That Cupid will impose for my neglect
Of his almighty dreadful little might.
Well, I will love, write, sigh, pray, sue, groan:
Some men must love my lady, and some Joan.

(III, i, 189–205)

There is no further evidence in the play that Rosaline is sexually promiscuous, but there is extended discussion of the relationship between blackness and beauty. The King and Berowne argue about it at some length:

King. By heaven, thy love is black as ebony.
Ber. Is ebony like her? O [wood] divine!
A wife of such wood were felicity.
O, who can give an oath? Where is a book?
That I may swear beauty doth beauty lack,
If that she learn not of her eye to look:
No face is fair that is not full so black.
King: O paradox! Black is the badge of hell,
The hue of dungeons, and the school of night;
And beauty's crest becomes the heavens well.
Ber. Devils soonest tempt, resembling spirits of light.
O, if in black my lady's brows be deck'd,
It mourns that painting [and] usurping hair
Should ravish doters with a false aspect:
And therefore is she born to make black fair.
Her favor turns the fashion of the days
For native blood is counted painting now;

And therefore red, that would avoid dispraise,
Paints itself black, to imitate her brow.

(IV, iii, 243–61)

This has a very close connection with Sonnet 127:

> In the old age black was not counted fair,
> Or if it were it bore not beauty's name;
> But now is black beauty's successive heir,
> And beauty slander'd with a bastard shame.
> For since each hand hath put on nature's power,
> Fairing the foul with art's false borrow'd face,
> Sweet beauty hath no name, no holy bow'r,
> But is profan'd, if not lives in disgrace.
> Therefore my mistress' eyes are raven black,
> Her brows so suited as they mourners seem
> At such who, not born fair, no beauty lack,
> Sland'ring creation with a false esteem:
>> Yet so they mourn, becoming of their woe,
>> That every tongue says beauty should look so.[10]

The argument here challenges the accepted notions of beauty. Black was formerly thought not beautiful, but now it has succeeded to (inherited) the aesthetic title because beauty itself has been bastardized by "art's false borrow'd face," i.e. cosmetics, toward which Shakespeare apparently had an almost obsessive aversion.[11]

Finally, since black is the color of mourning garments ("so suited"), it is fitting that the brows of the mistress are in mourning for all those beauties who are not so fortunate as she, but the result is that "every tongue" says that beauty should be like her. The first quatrain of Sonnet 132 amplifies the theme of dark eyes and mourning:

> Thine eyes I love, and they as pitying me,
> Knowing thy heart torment me with disdain,
> Have put on black, and loving mourners be,
> Looking with pretty ruth upon my pain.

---

[10]The *Love's Labor's Lost* passage seems to me to justify two emendations in line 10: the 1609 quarto reads "Her *eyes* so suited, *and* they mourners seem."

[11]He makes Hamlet burst out to Ophelia against "painting" at III, i, 142, and he denounces it again in the graveyard scene. Painting is associated with whores in *Measure for Measure* IV, iii, 38; and in *Cymbeline* III, iv, 50.

The resemblance between Rosaline and the Dark Lady of the sonnets gives us no help in identifying that mysterious person in real life, but in a sense it "distances" that figure in the sonnets. We do not try to find an Elizabethan lady who served as a model for Olivia in *Twelfth Night* or Imogen in *Cymbeline*. Rosaline in *Love's Labor's Lost* may be as fictional as her namesake in *Romeo and Juliet*, and so may her counterpart in the sonnets.

What does eventually emerge from a consideration of *Love's Labor's Lost* and the sonnets is that the drama, like the rest of the comedies, plays with the absurdity of lovers' extravagance. That there was an element of absurdity in Petrarchan sonnet making became evident soon after the vogue started in England. Jaques satirizes the lover "sighing like furnace, with a woeful ballad / Made to his mistress' eyebrow" (*As You Like It* II, vii, 148–49) and lest we put this down to Jaques' notorious cynicism, that of the exhausted debauchee according to Duke Senior, we have the amiable Amiens singing that most loving is mere folly. Duke Theseus of Athens would agree with him, for in the midst of his own wedding festivities he declares that the lover, like the lunatic and the poet, sees what is not really there—Helen's beauty in a brow of Egypt. He is as frantic (crazy) as the lunatic who sees more devils than vast hell can hold.

The sonnet's narrow room provides little space for the comic. Shakespeare can occasionally amuse himself (and perhaps some courtiers among his private friends) with obscene jokes like Sonnet 138, the Will sonnets, and Sonnet 151, but in general the sonnets are serious. The deflation of extravagant notions about love is left to the comic heroines, notably Rosalind. She corrects the legends about lovers who are supposed to have died for love, and she even gives practical advice to a beauty with black eyes and hair:

> No, faith, proud mistress, hope not after it.
> 'Tis not your inky brows, your black silk hair,
> Your bugle eyeballs, nor your cheek of cream
> That can entame my spirits to your worship.
> You foolish shepherd, wherefore do you follow her,
> Like foggy south, puffing with wind and rain?
> You are a thousand times a properer man
> Than she a woman. 'Tis such fools as you
> That makes the world full of ill-favor'd children.

'Tis not her glass, but you that flatters her,
And out of you she sees herself more proper
Than any of her lineaments can show her.
But, mistress, know yourself, down on your knees,
And thank heaven, fasting, for a good man's love;
For I must tell you friendly in your ear,
Sell when you can, you are not for all markets.

(*As You Like It* III, v, 45–60)

IV

In the foreground of a play the characters are what we see. They may suggest, or sometimes perhaps even represent, forces that are stronger than any person, but they must remain convincing as characters, resembling people in real life or people that might be in real life. But there is a background also. In *Romeo and Juliet* it is the night sky, filled with stars, which have a radiant beauty but may have a malevolent influence. Elizabeth Sewell has commented on the nature of the background in *A Midsummer Night's Dream*: "Behind these [the characters] the whole of nature is seen to be in movement. Everything is changing. The seasons change; the lovers exchange partners; myth itself may alter; 'Apollo flies, and Daphne holds the chase' (II, i, 231). The word 'change' comes round over and over again.

the spring, the summer,
The childing autumn, angry winter, change
Their wonted liveries . . .   (II, i, 111–13)

Run when you will; the story shall be changed: . . .   (II, i, 230)

O, Bottom, thou art chang'd; what do I see on thee?   (III, i, 115)
What change is this, sweet love?   (III, ii, 262)"[12]

The sonnets, too are full of references to change and transformation. This is partly the result of themes taken from Ovid, whose title *Metamorphoses* summarizes his elaborate poetic treatise on changes. Two of the sonnets in the Propagation Series deal eloquently with the theme of change. Number 12 makes a list of changes, in hours by the clock, in intervals of day and night, the fading violet and white hair of old age, the leafless tree that once gave shade to cattle, the harvest of

[12] *The Orphic Voice* (1961), p. 140.

grain that was once green; these observations make the poet wonder about the beauty of the Fair Friend

> That thou among the wastes of time must go,
> Since sweets and beauties do themselves forsake,
> And die as fast as they see others grow. . . .

Sonnet 15 develops a similar theme, that "every thing that grows / Holds in perfection but a little moment" and wasteful Time debates with decay over changing the day of youth to sullied night.

Many examples might be cited to show that change permeates the whole of the sonnets to the Fair Friend. The principal agent of change is of course Time, described in the second quatrain of 115:

> But reckoning Time, whose million'd accidents
> Creep in 'twixt vows, and change decrees of kings,
> Tan sacred beauty, blunt the sharp'st intents,
> Divert strong minds to th' course of alt'ring things . . .

But with all this there is the theme of resistance to change, especially when the change is mental or spiritual, not physical. "No, Time, thou shalt not boast that I do change" is the opening line of Sonnet 123. In some sonnets the assertion of constancy in love is related to the consistency of the poet's style:

> Why is my verse so barren of new pride?
> So far from variation or quick change?
> Why with the time do I not glance aside
> To new-found methods and to compounds strange?
> Why write I still all one, ever the same,
> And keep invention in a noted weed,
> That every word doth almost [tell] my name,
> Showing their birth, and where they did proceed?
> O know, sweet love, I always write of you,
> And you and love are still my argument;
> So all my best is dressing old words new,
> Spending again what is already spent:
> > For as the sun is daily new and old,
> > So is my love still telling what is told.

(76)

A recent commentary on this sonnet says "We move imperceptibly to the logical impossibilities inherent in the worship of a constant source,

a supernatural economy, something spent and saved too. This movement is sealed by the always potent image of the sun, with its intrinsic
association with the incarnate God: as the daily course of the sun
figures forth the death and resurrection of the Son in human hearts, so
'my love' is engaged in a continually renewed act of signification. . . .
The effect of the sonnet is to deify the poet's love." [13]

More simply, I would emphasize the way in which the contrast is
built up between "quick change," "variation," and "new pride" on
the one hand and that kind of constancy or permanence best expressed
in temporal terms. "Still" is a key word in this sonnet; it appears three
times, in line 5, line 10, and line 14. *Still* is a stronger word in
Shakespeare's language than it is in ours. It means "always,"
"forever." In one of the very few cases in which we can observe
Shakespeare speaking for himself and not through a character, we find
the word used in this sense: "Were my worth greater, my duety
would shew greater, meane time, as it is, it is bound to your Lordship;
To whom I wish long life *still* lengthned with all happinesse." [14]

The connection between the speaker's love and his poetry—they are
alike in their unchangeableness—is made evident again in Sonnet 105:

> Let not my love be call'd idolatry,
> Nor my belovëd as an idol show,
> Since all alike my songs and praises be
> To one, of one, still such, and ever so.
> Kind is my love to-day, to-morrow kind,
> Still constant in a wondrous excellence,
> Therefore my verse, to constancy confin'd,
> One thing expressing, leaves out difference.
> "Fair," "kind," and "true" is all my argument,
> "Fair," "kind," and "true," varying to other words,
> And in this change is my invention spent,
> Three themes in one, which wondrous scope affords,
>   "Fair," "kind," and "true" have often liv'd alone,
>   Which three till now never kept seat in one.

The implied accusation that such devoted love as is celebrated here is a
kind of idolatry is a commonplace. Shakespeare makes Juliet refer to it

---

[13]John D. Bernard, "'To Constancie Confin'de': The Poetics of Shakespeare's
Sonnets," *PMLA* 94 (1979): 82.
[14]Dedication to *The Rape of Lucrece*, 1594. *The Riverside Shakespeare*, p. 1,722.

when she is telling Romeo, in the balcony scene, what he may and may not swear by:

Jul. O, swear not by the moon, th'inconstant moon,
That monthly changes in her [circled] orb,
Lest that thy love prove likewise variable.
Rom. What shall I swear by?
Jul.   Do not swear at all;
Or if thou wilt, swear by thy gracious self,
Which is the god of my idolatry.

(II, ii, 109–14)

What seems, in the sonnet, like false logic ("I can't be an idolater because I worship only one god") may be based on the vague general notion current in Elizabethan times that religions other than Christianity were all polytheistic and therefore idolatrous. There may be awareness of the opposite notion, sometimes still maintained by Muslims, that Christians are idolators because they worship three gods. There certainly is reference to the doctrine of the Trinity in the poem but the tone is not, I think, religious. Booth quite rightly calls it a "playful experiment in perversity."[15] In line 11 the word *change* is important; it means of course "variation" or "modulation," as well as "inconstancy, fickleness" but may have association with *changes*, the different orders in which a peal of bells may be rung.

The affectation of simplicity and directness which is the burden of Sonnets 76 and 105 is not at all peculiar to Shakespeare. Sidney, for example, uses a very similar theme in sonnets 3 and 6 of *Astrophil and Stella*.

A special form of the theme of change brought about by time is the conventional topic of the seasons, appropriate enough in love poetry and prominent in *A Midsummer Night's Dream*. Titania makes much of the fact that the quarrel of the royal fairies has upset the natural course of the seasons:

we see

The seasons alter: hoary-headed frosts
Fall in the fresh lap of the crimson rose,
And on old Hiëms' [thin] and icy crown

---

[15] *Shakespeare's Sonnets* (1977), p. 336. Jane Roessner, in "Double Exposure: Shakespeare's Sonnets 100–114" (*ELH* 46 [1979]: 360–62) offers elaborate analysis of Sonnet 105, denying its playfulness and making it a metaphysical poem more complex than Donne's.

An odorous chaplet of sweet summer buds
Is, as in mockery, set; the spring, the summer,
The childing autumn, angry winter, change
Their wonted liveries, and the mazèd world,
By their increase, knows not which is which.

(II, i, 106–14)

The correspondence of the seasons to one's emotional states has been
noticed before, in Sonnets 97 ("How like a winter hath my absence
been") and 98 ("From you I have been absent in the spring"), but a
rather different, more literal, commentary on the cycle of the seasons
comes in the second and third quatrains of Sonnet 102:

Our love was new, and then but in the spring,
When I was wont to greet it with my lays,
As Philomel in summer's front doth sing,
And stops [her] pipe in growth of riper days:
Not that the summer is less pleasant now
Than when her mournful hymns did hush the night,
But that wild music burthens every bough,
And sweets grown common lose their dear delight.

This is part of an extended apology for not writing more frequently
and more assiduously. The nightingale (Philomela) ceases her singing
as summer comes on, so a poet may be justified in writing less. That
the songs of the nightingale could "hush the night" (presumably to
silence every other night sound because of their beauty) is evocative, as
is the line "But that wild music burthens every bough." *Burthens*
(burdens) means both "loads" and "provides choruses for."

Sonnet 104 has a similar reference to the passage of seasons as a mark
of the duration of love:

Three winters cold
Have from the forests shook three summers' pride,
Three beauteous springs to yellow autumn turn'd.
In process of the seasons have I seen,
Three April perfumes in three hot Junes burn'd,
Since first I saw you fresh, which yet are green.
Ah, yet doth beauty, like a dial hand,
Steal from his figure, and no pace perceiv'd,
So your sweet hue, which methinks still doth stand,
Hath motion, and mine eye may be deceiv'd.

(104.3–12)

Beauty is compared to the hand of a watch. A *dial* is not a sundial but a watch, like the one Touchstone drew from his pouch in the Forest of Arden when he moralized on the passage of time. The hand moves, although the spectator's eye cannot detect motion.

The last line quoted from Sonnet 104 ends "mine eye may be deceiv'd." This is a theme of *A Midsummer Night's Dream* as well. The juice of a little flower called "Love-in-Idleness" squeezed on the eyelids of a sleeping Athenian youth or maid or even on the Queen of Fairies can make the sleeper dote upon the first person seen upon awaking. Hermia says that she wishes her father looked but with her eyes, to which Theseus replies that her eyes must look with her father's judgment. At the end of the first scene the unhappy Helena soliloquizes upon her situation:

> Through Athens I am thought as fair as she.
> But what of that? Demetrius thinks not so;
> He will not know what all but he do know;
> And as he errs, doting on Hermia's eyes,
> So I, admiring of his qualities.
> Things base and vile, holding no quantity,
> Love can transpose to form and dignity.
> Love looks not with the eyes but with the mind;
> And therefore is wing'd Cupid painted blind.
>
> (I, i, 227–35)

The predominance of *eyes* in *A Midsummer Night's Dream* and the sonnets can even be shown statistically. The relative frequency of the word in *As You Like It* is .089; in *Much Ado* it is .052; in *Twelfth Night* it is .056. It is more important in *Love's Labor's Lost*, reaching a relative frequency of .152. But in *A Midsummer Night's Dream* it is .248 and in the sonnets it is .291.[16]

A pair of sonnets, 46 and 47, are based upon the *topos* of a war between the eyes and the heart. Characteristically, Shakespeare expresses this conflict not primarily with military imagery but with legal figures. The *mortal war* over how to divide the *conquest* of the sight of the beloved turns out to be a trial in court:

> Mine eye and heart are at a mortal war,
> How to divide the conquest of thy sight:
> Mine eye my heart [thy] picture's sight would bar,

---

[16]Martin Spevack, *A Complete and Systematic Concordance to the Works of Shakespeare* I and II, 1968.

> My heart mine eye the freedom of that right.
> My heart doth plead that thou in him dost lie
> (A closet never pierc'd with crystal eyes),
> But the defendant doth that plea deny,
> And says in him [thy] fair appearance lies.
> To ['cide] this title is impanellëd
> A quest of thoughts, all tenants to the heart,
> And by their verdict is determinëd
> The clear eye's moiety and the dear heart's part—
>> As thus: mine eye's due is [thy] outward part,
>> And my heart's right [thy] inward love of heart.

It is not quite clear, I think, whether the reader should take the word *picture* in line 3 as an actual portrait or not. Some editors so take it, but Shakespeare frequently means by it an image seen in the mind's eye. The heart can claim that the image is invisible because it lies in a *closet* (a small private room) never *pierc'd* (seen into) by *eyes,* which are transparent, like *crystal.* The *quest* (jury) of thoughts are all tenants of the heart and would, one might suppose, decide in the heart's favor. But the packed jury decides fairly: the visible features of the loved one are the share (*moiety*) of the eye and the inward traits are awarded to the heart.

Sonnet 47 continues the conceit, but the conflict is over:

> Betwixt mine eye and heart a league is took,
> And each doth good turns now unto the other;
> When that mine eye is famish'd for a look,
> Or heart in love with sighs himself doth smother,
> With my love's picture then my eye doth feast,
> And to the painted banquet bids my heart;
> Another time mine eye is my heart's guest,
> And in his thoughts of love doth share a part.
> So either by thy picture or my love,
> Thyself away are present still with me,
> For thou [not] farther than my thoughts canst move,
> And I am still with them, and they with thee;
>> Or if they sleep, thy picture in my sight
>> Awakes my heart to heart's and eye's delight.

A league is took means "a peace treaty has been signed." The eye and heart were formerly foes, in battle or in court, but now they are friends. They help each other, satisfying each other's needs in love. The hospitality images of *feast*, *banquet*, and *guest* emphasize the reconciliation. Even when the thoughts of the Fair Friend are asleep, the picture (which certainly sounds like an actual portrait here) arouses both the speaker's eye and heart to their delight.

Sonnet 24, on the other hand, clearly evokes not an actual portrait but an imagined one that figures in another discussion of the conflict between eye and heart:

> Mine eye hath play'd the painter and hath [stell'd]
> Thy beauty's form in table of my heart;
> My body is the frame wherein 'tis held,
> And perspective it is best painter's art.
> For through the painter must you see his skill,
> To find where your true image pictur'd lies,
> Which in my bosom's shop is hanging still,
> That hath his windows glazèd with thine eyes.
> Now see what good turns eyes for eyes have done:
> Mine eyes have drawn thy shape, and thine for me
> Are windows to my breast, wherethrough the sun
> Delights to peep, to gaze therein on thee.
>   Yet eyes this cunning want to grace their art,
>   They draw but what they see, know not the heart.

Inga-Stina Ewbank has called this sonnet "the Hamlet-like questioning of visual evidence,"[17] but it is also a little treatise on the ability of the eye to create, as a painter, and the limits of that ability. It can paint only the external appearance. S. Clark Hulse relates this idea to Castelvetro's theory of poetry and painting.[18]

Stell'd, which occurs elsewhere in Shakespeare, means "fixed" or perhaps "delineated"; *perspective* in line 4 means that kind of distortion which allows the true picture to be seen from only one particular standpoint, like the skull in Holbein's *The Ambassadors* in the National Gallery, London. Commentators cite a passage from *Richard II*:

---

[17] "'More Pregnantly than Words': Some Uses and Limitations of Visual Symbolism," *Shakespeare Survey* 24(1971): 16.

[18] "'A Piece of Skillful Painting' in Shakespeare's *Lucrece*," *Shakespeare Survey* 31 (1978): 18.

> For sorrow's eyes, glazëd with blinding tears,
> Divides one thing entire to many objects,
> Like perspectives, which rightly gaz'd upon
> Show nothing but confusion; ey'd awry
> Distinguish form. . . .

(II, ii, 16–20)

Lines 10–12 remain obscure for all the editors can do. How the Fair Friend's eyes can be, for the poet, windows to the poet's own breast, is one of those perspectives "which rightly gaz'd upon / Show nothing but confusion."

Sometimes the eye is not a painter but an alchemist, transmuting base things into noble, as in Sonnet 114:

> Or whether shall I say mine eye saith true,
> And that your love taught it this alcumy,
> To make of monsters and things indigest
> Such cherubins as your sweet self resemble,
> Creating every bad a perfect best
> As fast as objects to his beams assemble?

(114.3–8)

In the previous sonnet, 113, the speaker complains that his eye, which is supposed to have two functions, to receive images and to transmit them to the mind, in absence from the Friend performs only the first of these functions.

The corruption of the eye is a theme in two remarkable sonnets of the Dark Lady series. Since the eyes are part of the body, they, like every other part, can be corrupted. They are supposed to collect images and transmit them to the brain. They must see the truth, the fact, and report it. But what is the situation when they lie, reporting as true what is false? Sonnet 137 treats this situation:

> Thou blind fool, Love, what dost thou to mine eyes,
> That they behold and see not what they see?
> They know what beauty is, see where it lies,
> Yet what the best is take the worst to be.
> If eyes, corrupt by over-partial looks,
> Be anchor'd in the bay where all men ride,
> Why of eyes' falsehood hast thou forgëd hooks,
> Whereto the judgment of my heart is tied?
> Why should my heart think that a several plot,

93

Which my heart knows the wide world's common place?
Or mine eyes seeing this, say this is not,
To put fair truth upon so foul a face?
    In things right true my heart and eyes have erred,
    And to this false plague are they now transferred.[19]

The perjury of the eye is treated again in Sonnet 152, the last of the sonnets (in position in the Quarto if not in time) addressed to the Dark Lady. Here the inevitable punning of *eye-I* is quite serious. The first personal singular pronoun has become identical with the organ of vision, and that unified identity is a liar:

In loving thee thou know'st I am forsworn,
But thou art twice forsworn, to me love swearing;
In act thy bed-vow broke, and new faith torn
In vowing new hate after new love bearing.
But why of two oaths' breach do I accuse thee,
When I break twenty? I am perjur'd most,
For all my vows are oaths but to misuse thee,
And all my honest faith in thee is lost;
For I have sworn deep oaths of thy deep kindness,
Oaths of thy love, thy truth, thy constancy,
And to enlighten thee gave eyes to blindness,
Or made them swear against the thing they see;
    For I have sworn thee fair: more perjur'd eye,
    To swear against the truth so foul a lie![20]

V

Several thematic relationships between the sonnets and *The Merchant of Venice* depend upon the fact that the play of course deals with usury and the sonnets are full of figurative language which equates love (or, sometimes, sexual activity) with the lending of money and getting interest for it. In the sestet of Sonnet 9, for example ("Is it for fear to wet a widow's eye"), there is an argument that the spendthrift does less harm than the celibate:

---

[19]Michael J.B. Allen has a discussion of this sonnet in "Shakespeare's Man Descending a Staircase: Sonnets 126 to 154" in *Shakespeare Survey* 31 (1978), but Allen assumes, I think without warrant, that the sonnets are designed in groups of three and that there is interplay among members of a triad.

[20]Until recently most editors emended *eye* to *I* in line 13.

Look what an unthrift in the world doth spend,
Shifts but his place, for still the world enjoys it,
But beauty's waste hath in the world an end,
And kept unus'd, the user so destroys it:
    No love toward others in that bosom sits
    That on himself such murd'rous shame commits.

Look what means "whatever," and *his place* is in modern English "its place"; *murd'rous shame* is an Elizabethan construction for "shameful murder." In this passage the words *unus'd* and *user* have their ordinary meanings but also carry connotation of the word "usury."

That association becomes quite explicit in Sonnet 4, which is built almost entirely upon the ideas of spending, saving, hoarding, lending, giving, bequeathing, and the like:

Unthrifty loveliness, why dost thou spend
Upon thyself thy beauty's legacy?
Nature's bequest gives nothing, but doth lend,
And being frank she lends to those are free;
Then, beauteous niggard, why dost thou abuse
The bounteous largess given thee to give?
Profitless usurer, why dost thou use
So great a sum of sums, yet canst not live?
For having traffic with thyself alone,
Thou of thy self thy sweet self dost deceive,
Then how when Nature calls thee to be gone,
What acceptable audit canst thou leave?
    Thy unus'd beauty must be tomb'd with thee,
    Which usëd lives th' executor to be.

Line 4 means "And, being generous herself, she lends to those who are liberal and bountiful." *Live* in line 8 is a rhyme word, so its meaning may be imprecise, but it suggests (1) "gain a livelihood" and (2) "survive after death." *A sum of sums* has punning association with "some," as in Portia's description of herself:

I might in virtues, beauties, livings, friends,
Exceed account. But the full sum of me
Is sum of something.

                             (Merchant of Venice III, ii, 156–59)

95

In line 9 *traffic* means, as always in Shakespeare, "business" or "commerce"; it has no shade of the common modern meaning.

Another connection between the sonnets and the play has been pointed out by J. W. Lever: "In sonnets 133 and 134 ('Beshrew that heart that makes my heart to groan' and 'So now I have confessed that he is thine') there is an intrusion of dramatic conceits. The poet asks to go bail for his Friend and be imprisoned himself in the Mistress's 'steel bosom's ward'; he claims that the Friend merely stood as surety for the bond with which, like a usurer, she now binds him. These conceits recall actual plot situations in *The Merchant of Venice,* and the analogy is hardly a coincidence."[21]

There are a good many other passages which carry the atmosphere of *The Merchant of Venice* over into the sonnets, or vice versa, such as

> A day in April never came so sweet
> To show how costly summer was at hand
>
> (II, ix, 93–94)

which recalls Sonnet 3

> Thou art thy mother's glass, and she in thee
> Calls back the lovely April of her prime
>
> (9–10)

or Sonnet 98:

> From you I have been absent in the spring
> When proud-pied April (dress'd in all his trim)
>
> (1–2)

but these are atmospheric and might be considered merely part of the stock of Shakespeare's images of beauty.

A more significant relationship is pointed out by M. M. Mahood: "If generations of critics have been perplexed by the discrepancies between Shakespeare's apparent intentions in portraying Bassanio and the character who emerges from the play, the reason may be that Shakespeare's presentation of the character is related to a real-life discrepancy between what he wishes his friend to be and what he fears he is. So in the sonnets, with their many verbal parallels to *The Merchant of Venice*: Shakespeare strains in Sonnet 67 ("Ah, wherefore with infection should he live") and 68 ("Thus is his cheek the map of days outworn") to dissociate his friend from the corruption of the times and in Sonnet

---

[21] *The Elizabethan Love Sonnet* (1956), p. 180.

69 ("Those parts of thee that the world's eye doth view") blames those
times for adding to his friend's fair flower 'the rank smell of weeds';
yet the collection as a whole shows him to be haunted by the fear that
his friend is all the time a lily that festers.[22]

A consideration of the relationship between Antonio and Bassanio,
and whether it in any significant way parallels the relationship
between the poet and the Fair Friend, may be postponed for a moment. There is one connection that is very vivid and has no
dependence upon guesses about biographical background. It is the
meaning of Bassanio's soliloquy as he meditates on which of the
caskets to choose:

> The world is still deceived with ornament.
> In law, what plea so tainted and corrupt
> But, being season'd with a gracious voice,
> Obscures the show of evil? In religion,
> What damnëd error but some sober brow
> Will bless it, and approve it with a text,
> Hiding the grossness with fair ornament?
> There is no [vice] so simple but assumes
> Some mark of virtue on his outward parts.
> How many cowards, whose hearts are all as false
> As stairs of sand, wear yet upon their chins
> The beards of Hercules and frowning Mars,
> Who inward search'd, have livers white as milk,
> And these assume but valor's excrement
> To render them redoubted! Look on beauty
> And you shall see 'tis purchas'd by the weight,
> Which therein works a miracle in nature,
> Making them lightest that wear most of it.
> So are those crispëd snaky golden locks,
> Which [make] such wanton gambols with the wind
> Upon supposëd fairness, often known
> To be the dowry of a second head,
> The skull that bred them in the sepulchre.
> Thus ornament is but the guiled shore
> To a most dangerous sea; the beauteous scarf
> Veiling an Indian beauty; in a word,

---

[22]"Love's Confined Doom," *Shakespeare Survey* 15 (1962): 54.

> The seeming truth which cunning times put on
> To entrap the wisest.
>
> (III, ii, 74–101)

Many of these lines have counterparts in the sonnets. Sonnet 1 speaks of "the world's fresh ornament"; Sonnet 21 mentions a muse which "heaven itself for ornament doth use"; Sonnet 54 compares the external with the internal:

> O how much more doth beauty beauteous seem
> By that sweet ornament which truth doth give!

and Sonnet 70 declares that "The ornament of beauty is suspect." But it is Sonnet 68 which elaborates the figure of the wig:

> Thus is his cheek the map of days outworn,
> When beauty liv'd and died as flowers do now,
> Before these bastard signs of fair were born,
> Or durst inhabit on a living brow;
> Before the golden tresses of the dead,
> The right of sepulchres, were shorn away,
> To live a second life on second head;
> Ere beauty's dead fleece made another gay:
> In him those holy antique hours are seen,
> Without all ornament, itself and true,
> Making no summer of another's green,
> Robbing no old to dress his beauty new,
>   And him as for a map doth Nature store,
>   To show false Art what beauty was of yore.

Days outworn and *holy antique hours* are former times, characterized by simplicity and truth in contrast to modern artificiality and hypocrisy. *Beauty's dead fleece* carries suggestions of the Golden Fleece which Jason sought and found, and this image is prevalent in *The Merchant of Venice*:

>   her sunny locks
> Hang on her temples like a golden fleece
> Which makes her seat of Belmont Colchis' strond,
> And many Jasons come in quest of her.
>
> (I, i, 169–72)

Again in the third act, when Gratiano exults in the success he and his master enjoy in having won their ladies:

> How doth that royal merchant, good Antonio?
> I know he will be glad of our success;
> We are the Jasons, we have won the fleece.
>
> (III, ii, 239–41)

John Russell Brown sums it up in his New Arden edition of the play: "The two parts of the play are linked by these problems: Portia is the golden fleece, the merchants venture and hazard as any lover, the caskets deal all in value, the bond and the rings are pledges of possession. In the scramble of give and take, when appearance and reality are hard to distinguish, one thing seems certain: that giving is the most important part—giving prodigally, without thought for the taking."[23]

Some critics have seen in Sonnet 134 an odd but profound correspondence to the triangular situation of Antonio-Bassanio-Portia in the play.

> So now I have confess'd that he is thine,
> And I myself am mortgag'd to thy will,
> Myself I'll forfeit, so that other mine
> Thou wilt restore to be my comfort still.
> But thou wilt not, nor he will not be free,
> For thou art covetous, and he is kind;
> He learn'd but surety-like to write for me
> Under that bond that him as fast doth bind.
> The statute of thy beauty thou wilt take,
> Thou usurer, that put'st forth all to use,
> And sue a friend came debtor for my sake,
> So him I lose through my unkind abuse.
>   Him have I lost, thou hast both him and me,
>   He pays the whole, and yet I am not free.

There is obviously no one-to-one correlation here. Is the speaker Antonio, who offers to be sacrificed for his friend? But in line 7 the speaker seems to adopt a role more like that of Bassanio. And the usurer? In line 10 it would seem to be the lady—Portia, not Shylock? That way madness lies. Cyrus Hoy, who perceptively says that the triangle is like something in an Iris Murdoch novel, finds a solution: "the sadness Antonio feels at the virtual loss of his friend who is now turned lover represents the great area of feeling carried over direct and

---

[23]1955, p. lviii.

99

unchanged from life into the play. Antonio's sadness is the sadness of the poet in the sonnets when he contemplates the loss of the friend, but with the poet's grief and distress at the friend's unworthiness and the unworthiness of his chosen mistress refined away."[24]

The trouble with this conclusion is that when we first hear of it we have no reason to suppose that Antonio's sadness is caused by Bassanio's love for Portia. Antonio knows very little about it when the play opens with his

> In sooth, I know not why I am so sad;
> It wearies me, you say it wearies you;
> But how I caught it, found it, or came by it,
> What stuff 'tis made of, whereof it is born,
> I am to learn . . . .

(I, i, 1–5)

Salerio and Solanio think it is the worries of the merchant adventurer (often a symbolic equivalent of love in Shakespeare),[25] but Antonio denies it, and, as he also denies being in love, Solanio concludes by saying "Then let us say you are sad / Because you are not merry." If Shakespeare wished to have the audience believe that Antonio was sad because Portia was taking Bassanio away from him, he could surely have made it clear. Besides, it is conventional for a leading character to be sad at the beginning of a comedy. Duke Orsino is suffering from lover's melancholy at the beginning of *Twelfth Night*, and Rosalind is so sad at the beginning of *As You Like It* that Celia has much ado to make her merry.

It is of course true that Antonio and Bassanio have one of those Renaissance male friendships that have been surveyed in L.J. Mills's book, *One Soul in Bodies Twain* (1937). It is only the ignorant who call such relationships homosexual. But the sleuths who keep busy investigating the erotic-psychological background of the sonnets have noticed that there is another Antonio who has a marked fondness for a young man, in this case Sebastian, the twin brother of Viola in *Twelfth Night*. This proves nothing, because Antonio was a name Shakespeare rather fancied; there are Antonios in *Much Ado*, *Two Gentlemen of Verona,* and *The Tempest* who have nothing in common with the other two Antonios except their name.

---

[24]"Shakespeare and the Revenge of Art," *Rice University Studies* 60 (1974): 82.
[25]For example, *Romeo and Juliet* II, ii, 82–84; *Two Gentlemen of Verona* II, iv, 168–71; *Troilus and Cressida* I, i. 98–104.

VI

The connection between the sonnets and *All's Well That Ends Well* has been noticed by the critics, especially Muriel Bradbrook, Cyrus Hoy, and Roger Warren.[26] The concern of these critics, however, has been to explicate, and in some respects to defend, *All's Well*, usually regarded as one of Shakespeare's least successful comedies. Professor Bradbrook, for example, maintains that "Helena's speech to the Countess (I, iii, 191–217) is the poetic center of the play, but the structural center is the King's judgement on virtue and nobility. For once, the dramatist and the poet in Shakespeare were pulling different ways. *All's Well That Ends Well* expresses in its title a hope that is not fulfilled; all did not end well, and it is not a successful play.'' Our interest here is rather the reverse: to see whether the play casts any light on the sonnets.

If one assumes that the sonnets are more subjective, more direct expressions of feeling and thought than the play, since the play is after all a dramatization of a tale of Boccaccio by way of Painter's *Palace of Pleasure*, then it would seem to be more difficult to learn anything about the sonnets from examining the play. But as it has been suggested that the sonnets are in some sense dramatic, an examination of the strains common to play and poems may be profitable.

Sonnet 57 develops a conventional theme, that being in love is a kind of slavery:

> Being your slave, what should I do but tend
> Upon the hours and times of your desire?
> I have no precious time at all to spend
> Nor services to do, till you require.
> Nor dare I chide the world-without-end hour,
> Whilst I, my sovereign, watch the clock for you,
> Nor think the bitterness of absence sour,
> When you have bid your servant once adieu.
> Nor dare I question with my jealous thought
> Where you may be, or your affairs suppose,

---

[26]M. C. Bradbrook, "Virtue is the True Nobility: A Study of the Structure of *All's Well That Ends Well*," *RES* n.s.1 (1950): 289–301; and *Shakespeare and Elizabethan Poetry* (1951), 162–70. Cyrus Hoy, "Shakespeare and the Revenge of Art," *Rice University Studies* 60 (1974): 71–94. Roger Warren, "Why Does It End Well? Helena, Bertram, and the Sonnets," *Shakespeare Survey* 22 (1969): 79–82; and "'A Lover's Complaint,' 'All's Well,' and The Sonnets," *N&Q* 215 (1970): 130–32.

> But like a sad slave stay and think of nought
> Save where you are how happy you make those.
> So true a fool is love that in your will
> (Though you do any thing) he thinks no ill.

The sonnet is full of dependent clauses and phrases, so that the grammatical structure reinforces the theme of dependency. The monotonous monosyllables of lines 11 and 13 produce an effect of glum resignation to the slave-fool role the speaker declares he is playing. The opening question, apparently rhetorical, turns out to be answerable by a series of negatives: *no . . . time . . . to spend, Nor services to do, Nor dare I, Nor think, Nor dare I question*, leading up to the positive "But like a sad slave stay and think of nought." There is much in this sonnet about *thinking* and *thought; chiding the time* and *questioning* the place—these functions of *my jealious thought*. Finally, in *thinks no ill*, the speaker is such a fool in love that he makes no moral judgment on the beloved's behavior.

Helena's confession to the Countess of her love for Bertram is equally humble:

> Then I confess
> Here on my knee, before high heaven and you,
> That before you, and next unto high heaven,
> I love your son.
> My friends were poor, but honest, so's my love.
> Be not offended, for it hurts not him
> That he is lov'd of me; I follow him not
> By any token of presumptuous suit,
> Nor would I have him till I do deserve him,
> Yet never know how that desert should be.
> I know I love in vain, strive against hope;
> Yet in this captious and intenible sieve
> I still pour in the waters of my love
> And lack not to lose still. Thus Indian-like,
> Religious in mine error, I adore
> The sun, that looks upon his worshipper,
> But knows of him no more.

(I, iii, 192–207)

Though Professor Bradbrook calls this speech "the poetic centre of the play," it is at first plain, simple and direct. Its primary function is to characterize Helena. Only at the end, when she likens her love for Bertram to water poured into a sieve, and her relationship to him to that of the superstitious Indian sun-worshipper, do we get anything that approaches the poetry of the sonnets. But Sonnet 57 begins with poetic bravura and does not swerve from it. The speaker is not characterized. What can be made of slavery, thought, and absence is the sole concern of the sonnet. That this is not an insignificant game is made manifest by the fact that Sonnet 58 is an exercise on the same theme or themes:

> That god forbid that made me first your slave
> I should in thought control your times of pleasure,
> Or at your hand th'account of hours to crave,
> Being your vassal bound to stay your leisure.
> O, let me suffer (being at your beck)
> Th'imprison'd absence of your liberty,
> And patience, tame to sufferance, bide each check,
> Without accusing you of injury.
> Be where you list, your charter is so strong,
> That you yourself may privilege your time
> To what you will, to you it doth belong
> Yourself to pardon of self-doing crime.
>> I am to wait, though waiting so be hell,
>> Not blame your pleasure, be it ill or well.

This sonnet, less harmonious in tone than its companion, is not based on modest negatives. Its focus seems to be on the second person pronoun. The first six lines have *your* in every line, and after line 7 we get the crowded *you . . . you . . . your . . . you yourself . . . your . . . you . . . you . . . Yourself to pardon of self-doting crime.* In all this spate of second-person pronouns, the *I* and *me* become almost imperceptible. The sonnet is far more conceited and abstract than the language of Helena. The second quatrain is particularly compact: the speaker wishes to suffer *Th'imprison'd absence of your liberty*, which would unravel to something like "Your absence confines and punishes me as if I were in prison, but that absence gives you *liberty*" ("freedom," of course, but perhaps also some suggestion of libertine behaviour, as in the opening line of Sonnet 41: "Those pretty wrongs that liberty commits").

There are passages in *All's Well* that deal with imaginary sight, the ability to visualize in absence the features of a loved person. Helena, in her first soliloquy, says she cannot remember her father, the famous physician:

>   I think not on my father.
> And these great tears grace his remembrance more
> Than those I shed for him. What was he like?
> I have forgot him. My imagination
> Carries no favor in't but Bertram's.
> I am undone, there is no living, none,
> If Bertram be away. 'Twere all one
> That I should love a bright particular star
> And think to wed it, he is so above me.
> . . . . 'Twas pretty, though a plague,
> To see him every hour, to sit and draw
> His archëd brows, his hawking eye, his curls,
> In our heart's table—heart too capable
> Of every line and trick of his sweet favor.
> But now he's gone, and my idolatrous fancy
> Must sanctify his reliques.

                                          (I, i, 79–87, 92–98)

Several passages in the sonnets are close to this in concept or in diction. The first quatrain of Sonnet 24, for example, already cited in connection with the eyes imagery in *A Midsummer Night's Dream*, makes the eye a painter of the Fair Friend's portrait.

Sonnets 113 ("Since I left you, mine eye is in my mind") and 114 ("Or whether doth my mind being crown'd with you") deal with a similar conceit, and Roger Warren finds comparable passages in Sonnets 27 and 31. In the first of these the speaker is unable to sleep at night but looks at "darkness which the blind do see."

> Save that my soul's imaginary sight
> Presents [thy] shadow to my sightless view,
> Which like a jewel hung in ghastly night,
> Makes black night beauteous, and her old face new.

In the second, there is a remarkable conjunction of tears for the dead and the imagined image of the living loved one:

> How many a holy and obsequious tear
> Hath dear religious love stol'n from mine eye
> As interest of the dead, which now appear
> But things remov'd that hidden in [thee] lie!

That *All's Well*, like *Romeo and Juliet*, is related to the sonnets is suggested again by the fact that Helena's letter to the countess of Rossillion, after her departure from the court, is in the form of a sonnet. She identifies herself as a pilgrim, and she sounds like the poet addressing the Fair Friend when she says

> Ambitious love hath so in me offended
> That barefoot plod I the cold ground upon
> With sainted vow my faults to have amended.
>
> (III, iv, 5–7)

If Helena's speech sometimes resembles the language of the sonnets, reflecting the poet's feelings about himself and the Fair Friend, is Bertram then some version of that Fair Friend? Cyrus Hoy thinks so: "Helena is a triumph of dramatic portraiture, but no one has ever said so much for Bertram, and here is where the dramatist's art has always seemed to most critics to falter, though I suspect the dramatist's art may not have faltered so much as it rebelled. Bertram is the young man of the sonnets in his most unattractive aspects; the dramatist seems to have declined to give him any qualities that would modify Parolles' description of him (at IV, iii, 220) as a 'dangerous and lascivious boy.'"[27] The Fair Friend is surely not summed up in Parolles' words, and as for Bertram, the conclusion of Geoffrey Bullough states the matter well: "Bertram is one of Shakespeare's first attempts to portray a man of spoiled excellence. 'Lilies that fester smell far worse than weeds,' and we should not forget his few good qualities."[28]

VII

A remarkable speech near the very beginning of *Measure for Measure* is put into the mouth of the Duke as he prepares to turn over his authority to Angelo. Dramatically, it is an example of the misleading first appearance, which Shakespeare uses often, in *Macbeth*, in *Anthony and Cleopatra*, in *The Winter's Tale* and elsewhere. The Duke says that there is a kind of *character* in Angelo's life (i.e., "outward marks bespeaking inward qualities" Schmidt 2) that gives the observer the true knowledge of the man. But then he goes on to describe, in a didactic and poetic way, the need for virtue to be exercised, put to use:

---

[27]*Op. cit.*, p. 87.
[28]*Narrative and Dramatic Sources of Shakespeare* (1958), 2: 386.

> Thyself and thy belongings
> Are not thine own so proper as to waste
> Thyself upon thy virtues, they on thee
>
> (I, i, 29–31)

"Spirits are not finely touched," he says, "but to fine issues." Walter Whiter in the eighteenth century noticed that the passage reflects language and images from two passages in the Book of Luke.[29] The word *belongings* in line 29 means the same thing as *virtues* in line 31. In the Bible passage Jesus says that he was touched and felt the *virtue* gone out of him. We would now translate *virtue* as "mana," but the Elizabethans lacked that word.

In a curious way, the self-sufficiency which is an attribute of Angelo in the early part of *Measure for Measure* suggests the octave of Sonnet 94 ("They that have pow'r to hurt and will do none"). He is such a paragon at the beginning of the play; he is urged, however, to put forth his virtues, his "belongings," and the ironic result is that he loses his self-sufficiency and becomes a lily that festers.

Isabella discourses eloquently on the subject of authority when she is pleading with Angelo to save her brother's life:

> O, it is excellent
> To have a giant's strength, but it is tyrannous
> To use it like a giant.
>
> (II, ii, 107–09)

> . . . man, proud man,
> Dress'd in a little brief authority,
> Most ignorant of what he's most assur'd,
> (His glassy essence), like an angry ape
> Plays such fantastic tricks before high heaven
> As makes the angels weep;
>
> (II, ii, 117–22)

She challenges him to look into his own heart and see if he cannot be tempted as Claudio was; as she says it, he is tempted. He says, aside:

> She speaks, and 'tis
> Such sense that my sense breeds with it.
>
> (II, ii, 141–42)

The first *sense* means "meaning" and the second "sensuality," as in a later line when he asks

---

[29]*A Specimen of a Commentary on Shakespeare*, ed. Alan Over and Mary Bell (1967), pp. 203–04.

106

> Can it be
> That modesty may more betray our sense
> Than woman's lightness?
>
> (II, ii, 167–69)

The same multiple meaning of *sense* may be observed in the sonnets to the Fair Friend:

> All men make faults, and even I in this,
> Authorizing thy trespass with compare,
> Myself corrupting, salving thy amiss,
> Excusing [thy] sins more than [thy] sins are;
> For to thy sensual fault I bring in sense. . . .
>
> (35.5–9)

There is some punning relationship between *sins* and *sense* (*sensual*) here, though the primary meaning of *sense* in line 9 is "reason."

Another meaning of the multi-faceted word *sense* is dominant in one of the Dark Lady sonnets, 141:

> In faith, I do not love thee with mine eyes,
> For they in thee a thousand errors note,
> But 'tis my heart that loves what they despise,
> Who in despite of view is pleas'd to dote;
> Nor are mine ears with thy tongue's tune delighted,
> Nor tender feeling to base touches prone,
> Nor taste, nor smell, desire to be invited
> To any sensual feast with thee alone;
> But my five wits nor my five senses can
> Dissuade one foolish heart from serving thee,
> Who leaves unsway'd the likeness of a man,
> Thy proud heart's slave and vassal wretch to be:
>   Only my plague thus far I count my gain,
>   That she that makes me sin awards me pain.

The curious logic of this sonnet maintains that the Dark Lady does not dominate the speaker's sight, hearing, taste, smell or touch. The *five wits* are not specified, but it was possession of all of them that indicated sanity to the Elizabethans. "Bless thy five wits!" exclaims Edgar in the hovel scene when it is clear that Lear is mad. The Dark Lady's *proud heart* has subdued the speaker's *foolish heart* to the condition of slavery, leaving him the mere *likeness of a man*. His consolation is a paradox in the couplet: his *plague* (loving her) is a *gain* because in making him *sin* she simultaneously awards him punishment for it (*pain*).

VIII

Connections between the sonnets and the plays are particularly strong in an early tragedy, *Romeo and Juliet*, and a history play, *Henry IV, Part II*. *Romeo and Juliet* is, indeed, a play written by a sonneteer. Not only is the prologue before Act I a sonnet; it is a summary of the plot of the play, an explanation of the prime force at work in it (the hero and heroine are star-crossed lovers) and a description of the mood it intends to evoke:

> From forth the fatal loins of these two foes
> A pair of star-cross'd lovers take their life;
> Whose misadventur'd piteous overthrows
> Doth with their death bury their parents' strife.
> The fearful passage of their death-mark'd love,
> And the continuance of their parents' rage,
> Which, but their childrens' end, nought could remove,
> Is now the two hours' traffic of our stage. . . .

The misadventur'd piteous outcome is in no doubt; the fearful passage contains no suspense except that of how and when the death-mark'd climax will take place. To be sure, the hero changes radically and so does the heroine—all in Act I, the end of which requires another sonnet spoken by the Chorus to introduce the new situation. That chorus is filled with conceits which are the very stuff of Shakespeare's sonnets:

> Now old desire doth in his death-bed lie,
> And young affection gapes to be his heir; . . .

Inheritance and bequests figure prominently in the sonnets, especially the first seventeen. Images of fair and fair (two different things), bewitching by the charm of looks, baited hooks, passion and power, the vows sworn by lovers—all these are the common fabric of the sonnets and appear (or reappear) in the Prologue to Act II.

Within Act I the beginning of the love between Romeo and Juliet is expressed in a sonnet shared between them:

> *Rom.* If I profane with my unworthiest hand
> This holy shrine, the gentle sin is this,
> My lips, two blushing pilgrims, ready stand
> To smooth that rough touch with a tender kiss.

> *Jul.* Good pilgrim, you do wrong your hand too much,
>   Which mannerly devotion shows in this:
>   For saints have hands that pilgrims' hands do touch,
>   And palm to palm is holy palmers' kiss.
> *Rom.* Have not saints lips, and holy palmers too?
> *Jul.* Ay, pilgrim, lips that they must use in pray'r.
> *Rom.* O then, dear saint, let lips do what hands do,
>   They pray—grant thou, lest faith turn to despair.
> *Jul.* Saints do not move, though grant for prayers' sake.
> *Rom.* Then move not while my prayer's effect I take.
>
> (I, v, 93–106)

Winifred Nowottny has commented on this passage:

It might be objected that an elaborate style will do for a sonneteer but not for a dramatist. There is, however, a very good reason why Romeo the lover, and Juliet, too, should talk like a sonneteer. The play was written in the heyday of the sonnet, and the language of the sonnet was the language of love. The kind of love Petrarch had celebrated was often regarded as an experience which lifted a man above himself, as an exaltation of the spirit so spectacular that only religious experience could compete with it for intensity. It would hardly have been possible for Shakespeare, writing about idealistic passion when the sonnet vogue was at its height, to ignore the sonneteer's language for it. And indeed, the convention was very useful for his purposes. The fact that it was, at this time, so highly developed, made it possible for him to present the experience of his hero and heroine in language which could claim to be universal; it is the language of lovers in general, not of Romeo and Juliet in particular; they do not need individual characters in order to be able to speak as they do. Nonetheless, they are sufficiently individualized, within the world of the play itself, by the fact that to be in their state of mind is to be in a world of one's own. Their world, to Mercutio, is absurd; it is a closed world to the Nurse; it is a world Capulet has no time for, and one of whose willfulness the Friar disapproves.[30]

Anything important, to be fully realized, must be viewed both tragically and comically. At least it is so in Shakespeare. Therefore Mercutio and his attitude toward lovers and particularly to lovers as poets: "Now is he for the numbers that Petrarch flow'd in. Laura to his lady was a kitchen wench (marry, she had a better love to berhyme

---

[30] "Shakespeare's Tragedies" in *Shakespeare's World*, ed. James Sutherland and Joel Hurstfield (1964), p. 50.

her), Dido a dowdy, Cleopatra a gypsy, Helen and Hero hildings and harlots, Thisby a grey eye or so, but not to the purpose" (II, iv, 38–43). It is the only reference to Petrarch in all of Shakespeare.

In the ironic opening of the last act of *Romeo and Juliet*, just before he hears the mistaken but tragic news of Juliet's death, Romeo tells of a dream he had:

> If I may trust the flattering truth of sleep,
> My dreams presage some joyful news at hand.
> My bosom's lord sits lightly in his throne,
> And all this day an unaccustom'd spirit
> Lifts me above the ground with cheerful thoughts.
> I dreamt my lady came and found me dead—
> Strange dream, that gives a dead man leave to think!
> And breath'd such life with kisses in my lips
> That I reviv'd and was an emperor.
>
> (V, i, 1–9)

This is reminiscent of the couplet of Sonnet 87:

> Thus have I had thee as a dream doth flatter:
> In sleep a king, but waking no such matter.

One of the sonnets on absence, 27, pictures the speaker as sleepless at night,

> Looking on darkness which the blind do see;
> Save that my soul's imaginary sight
> Presents [thy] shadow to my sightless view,
> Which like a jewel hung in ghastly night,
> Makes black night hideous, and her old face new.
>
> (8–12)

The atmosphere is not unlike that of Romeo's first exclamation about Juliet:

> O, she doth teach the torches to burn bright!
> It seems she hangs upon the cheek of night
> As a rich jewel in an Ethiop's ear—
> Beauty too rich for use, for earth too dear!
>
> (I, v, 44–47)

Friar Lawrence, who is an authority on herbs and their various uses, is not unacquainted with the standard controversy about whether the origin of love is in the eyes or in the heart, a conflict which is the substance of Sonnets 46 and 47. When he hears of Romeo's sudden change from Rosaline to Juliet, he exclaims:

> Holy Saint Francis, what a change is here!
> Is Rosaline, that thou didst love so dear,
> So soon forsaken? Young men's love then lies
> Not truly in their hearts, but in their eyes.

(II, iii, 65–68)

One could easily go through the play and pick out phrases which might have come from the sonnets. *The worshipp'd sun; my wearied self; As is the bud bit with an envious worm; when she dies, with beauty dies her store; Let two more summers wither in their pride; When well-apparell'd April on the heel / Of limping winter treads; When the devout religion of mine eye*—all occur in the first two scenes of Act I.[31]

It is more surprising that the sonnets have much in common with *Henry IV, Part II*. Yet it should not surprise us if we realize that the play and the poems share two major subjects: the rejection of a friend and the tyranny of time. Sonnet 49 strangely predicts, or supposes the possibility, of a rejection of the poet by the Fair Friend at some future time:

> Against that time (if ever that time come)
> When I shall see thee frown on my defects,
> When as thy love hath cast his utmost sum,
> Call'd to that audit by advis'd respects;
> Against that time when thou shalt strangely pass,
> And scarcely greet me with that sun, thine eye,
> When love converted from the thing it was
> Shall reasons find of settled gravity;
> Against that time do I insconce me here
> Within the knowledge of mine own desert,
> And this my hand against myself uprear,
> To guard the lawful reasons on thy part.
>> To leave poor me thou hast the strength of laws,
>> Since why to love I can allege no cause.

---

[31]The fullest treatment of the relationship of the sonnets to *Romeo and Juliet* is Inge Leimberg, *Shakespeares Romeo und Julia: Von der Sonettdichtung zur Liebestragödie*, München, 1968.

Three quatrains all beginning with *Against that time* form a kind of
forbidding litany. *Against* means "in anticipation of," as it does in the
first line of Sonnet 63, "Against my love shall be as I am now," but it
also has an ironic suggestion of the prepositional meaning, "in opposition to." The first two quatrains have the following word "when,"
with decreasing uncertainty, but the third sounds positive. *I do insconce
me here* is to shelter, hide, or protect myself, as Falstaff insconces himself behind the arras in *The Merry Wives* to avoid being seen by Mistress Page. But the poet says he insconces himself within the knowledge of what he deserves. Lines 5 and 6 have reminded many readers of
Prince Hal's (or rather King Henry V's) rejection of Falstaff. Another
passage in the play is evoked by lines 7 and 8. Early in *2 Henry IV* the
Chief Justice, chiding Falstaff, says, "There is not a white hair in your
face but should have its effect of gravity," to which Falstaff replies
"His effect of gravy, gravy, gravy." *Casting his utmost sum* and *audit*
suggest that the love is quantitative and measurable, the kind that
King Lear tragically expects from his daughters. *Advised respects* means
"cold, careful calculations"; a passage in *King John* illustrates:

> to know the meaning
> Of dangerous majesty, when perchance it frowns
> More upon humor than advis'd respect.
>
> (IV, ii, 212–14)

As L. C. Knights has observed, the dominant tone of *2 Henry IV* is
also characteristic of many of the sonnets.[32] This is particularly true of
passages dealing with time. In Act III, scene i, the old king, suffering
from insomnia, is greeted in the morning by three of his courtiers who
have come to consult on matters of state. He is in a despairing mood
about the passage of time:

> O God, that one might read the book of fate,
> And see the revolution of the times
> Make mountains level, and the continent,
> Weary of solid firmness, melt itself
> Into the sea, and other times to see
> The beachy girdle of the ocean
> Too wide for Neptune's hips; how chance's mocks

---

[32]"Time's Subjects: The Sonnets and *Henry IV, Part II,*" *Some Shakespearean
Themes* (1959), pp. 45–64.

And changes fill the cup of alteration
With divers liquors! O, if this were seen,
The happiest youth, viewing his progress through,
What perils past, what crosses to ensue,
Would shut the book, and sit him down and die.

(III, i, 45–56)

Sonnet 64 is a similar meditation:

When I have seen by Time's fell hand defaced
The rich proud cost of outworn buried age;
When sometime lofty towers I see down rased,
And brass eternal slave to mortal rage;
When I have seen the hungry ocean gain
Advantage on the kingdom of the shore;
And the firm soil win of the wat'ry main,
Increasing store with loss, and loss with store;
When I have seen such interchange of state,
Or state itself confounded to decay,
Ruin hath taught me thus to ruminate,
That Time will come and take my love away.
    This thought is as a death, which cannot choose
    But weep to have that which it fears to lose.

The sonnet exhibits striking contrasts: pounding monosyllables, as in the first four feet of the first line and all of the last line, with polysyllabic variations—*outworn, buried, advantage, increasing, interchange, confounded.* The poem is what its neighbor, 65, calls a "fearful meditation." *Brass eternal,* the Horatian phrase for durability, becomes the *slave* to *mortal* (deadly) *rage.* The war between shore and sea leads to the abstraction *interchange of state,* where *state* means "condition" but also suggests "nation" and the political concern that so troubles King Henry IV. Wordplay on *ruin* leads to *ruminate,* and this in turn provides the basis for a comparison of a thought with death.

Other passages in *II Henry IV* suggest the same concerns that we find in the sonnets. Hastings, at a meeting of the conspirators against King Henry, says "We are time's subjects, and time bids be gone" (I, iii, 110). Prince Hal says to Poins, "thus we play the fools with the time, and the spirits of the wise sit in the clouds and mock us" (II, ii, 142).

B. T. Spencer describes the central theme of the play:

113

Though shades and variations in its purport are present—it is sometimes the challenger of human desires, sometimes an intruder into the human scene from another realm, sometimes an inscrutable enemy thwarting human hopes, sometimes a maze through which blinded man stumbles to frustration —inclusively time is regarded as something against which man must pit himself. It is a hovering, a relentless agent in human affairs. Therefore, Hal's rejection of Falstaff, as the crucial scene in the drama, cannot well be interpreted apart from so persistent a theme. In fact, it is the frame of reference in which the drama is set. In other words, the subject of *2 Henry IV* is man against time.[33]

The topic is also a major theme of the sonnets. It occupies the foreground of 12, 15, 19, 55, 59, 60, 65, 68, and no doubt many others.

---

[33] "2 *Henry IV* and the Theme of Time," *UTQ* 13 (1943–44): 397.

CHAPTER FIVE

Order and Punctuation

S ince the sonnets, as they were published in 1609, are numbered, from 2 to 154, (116 being misnumbered 119) it is natural to regard them offhand as a sequence, designed to be read in order, as Spenser's *Amoretti* are. But there are some signs of disarrangement, and many editors have attempted to rearrange them in what they suppose to be the original order, the order in which they were written or the order in which they would have appeared in Shakespeare's manuscript if he had taken it to Richard Field to be printed, as he took *Venus and Adonis* and *The Rape of Lucrece*. Hyder Rollins, in his Variorum edition of the sonnets in 1944, compiled a table showing the rearrangement in twenty editions, from John Benson's in 1640 to Tucker Brooke's in 1936.[1] Rollins also surveyed, with what seems like incredible patience, the arguments used to support each reordering and the arguments (sometimes mere assertions) to support the 1609 order as the one closest to the poet's intention. Rollins' display, which might, one would think, have amounted to a demonstration of the futility of attempting to solve the problem, did nothing of the kind. The rearrangements, and the defenses of the quarto order, have continued. To explain this, we should perhaps recognize that what looks like a puzzle always attracts solvers, and that enough of a child's fascination with narrative remains in us so that we wish to have a story even if we are reminded over and over that sonnets (in the 1590s, anyway) are not narrative poems.

L. C. Knights puts the matter in another way: "As everyone knows, the Sonnets contain a number of themes that seem to issue directly from the life history of the poet; and if we make a prose paraphrase of the poems in the order in which they appeared in Thorpe's edition of 1609 we can piece together a story that has a tantalizing appearance of

---

[1] *The Variorum Shakespeare: The Sonnets* (1944) 2: 113–16.

fragmentary autobiography." If that is so of the 1609 order, it may be even more true of a rearrangement. But first of all let us note that there is nothing whatever in "the life history of the poet" as we know it from records that has a direct bearing on the themes of the sonnets. The supposed life story is deduced from the poems and then used to interpret them. As Knights remarks, "There are various reasons for not finding this an entirely satisfactory procedure."[2]

But let us see what kind of story results. John Dover Wilson thought that Sonnet 59 is the first of a dozen sonnets based on Ovid's *Metamorphoses*, all written while Shakespeare was traveling on a two-months' journey in August-September, 1597, when the theaters were closed by the Privy Council because of the production of a seditious play, *The Isle of Dogs*, at the Swan Theater.[3] The story situation, as Wilson would have it, goes something like this: The tyranny of cyclical repetition leads to a meditation on the Fair Friend's earlier appearance in history (59) and the poet's ability to preserve him in verse (60). The image of the Friend keeps the poet awake at night when they are separated (61); their separation is not only geographical, but chronological (62). But, as the Fair Friend grows old, like the poet, his youthful beauty will be preserved by the poet's verse (63). The thought of the ruins of time leads to the thought of the loss of the Fair Friend (64), but there is the possibility that the miracle of poetry will preserve him (65). The world is so bad that the poet would gladly leave it, except for deserting the Fair Friend (66). Why should the Fair Friend go on living in such a bad world? To show what Nature could formerly boast of (67). In fact, the Fair Friend is a kind of map, showing the modern artificial world what natural beauty was like (68). Modern eyes can see the Fair Friend's beauty, but within they suspect corruption (69). This is not surprising, for beauty always arouses envy; if it were not so, the Friend would rule over a kingdom of hearts (70).

Some of these sonnets seem clearly linked: 59 ("If there be nothing new, but that which is / Hath been before") and 60 ("Like as the waves make toward the pibled shore") are connected by theme and logic. Sixty-two and 63 deal with age and survival. Sixty-four and 65

---

[2]*Some Shakespearean Themes* (1959), p. 46.
[3]See William Ingram, *A London Life in the Brazen Age: Francis Langley, 1548-1602.* (1978), pp. 168–69.

are further meditations on Time's fell hand. Sixty-six, 67 and 68 are complaints about these bad days, and 69 and 70 refer to the slander on the Friend, that he is beautiful but has grown, or may grow, common.

The connections between the linked pairs are less clear. Furthermore, although 59 and 60 are congenial neighbors, 59 has something in common with 106:

> O that recórd could with backward look,
> Even of five hundreth courses of the sun,
> Show me your image in some antique book,
> Since mind at first in character was done!
>
> (59.5–8)

and

> When in the chronicle of wasted time
> I see descriptions of the fairest wights,
> And beauty making beautiful old rhyme
> In praise of ladies dead and lovely knights,
> Then in the blazon of sweet beauty's best,
> Of hand, of foot, of lip, of eye, of brow,
> I see their antique pen would have expressed
> Even such a beauty as you master now.
>
> (106.1–8)

Equally striking is the resemblance between the end of Sonnet 69

> To thy fair flower add the rank smell of weeds;
> But why thy odor matcheth not thy show,
> The [soil] is this, that thou dost common grow.

and the couplet of Sonnet 94:

> For sweetest things turn sourest by their deeds,
> Lilies that fester smell far worse than weeds.[4]

Yet Sonnet 94 has strong thematic links with Sonnet 93. According to Brents Stirling, whose rearrangement of the Dark Lady sonnets Dover Wilson accepted, nearly three fourths of the sonnets are linked "inviolably" with at least one other adjacent sonnet.[5]

---

[4]This last line of course appears also in *Edward III*, an apocryphal play which some (e.g., Kenneth Muir) think Shakespeare had some hand in.
[5]*The Shakespeare Sonnet Order: Poems and Groups* (1968), p. 18.

So the rearranger's hands are sometimes tied. But Stirling proceeds to reconstruct a poem, which he calls C of Group II, about sleep and absence which goes as follows: The poet, wakeful, questions whether it is the Fair Friend or himself that is the cause of his insomnia (61). He elaborates on his wakefulness (27) and continues to compare what he owes to day and to night (28), but he finally concludes that seeing the Fair Friend in dreams is better than not seeing him in the daytime (43). Here is his justification: "These unifying elements of theme, diction, and structure are more than enough to outweigh a literalist's objection that 61, 17, and 28 describe a poet open-eyed and cursed with insomnia, while 43 describes one who 'winks,, who is sound asleep. 'Contradictions' like this are not uncommon in the Sonnets . . . In any event, it is the *eye* that wakes during the broken slumber of the earlier sonnets (61.1-4, 10; 27.7-10), and it is still the eye that sees so piercingly while the poet sleeps in 43."

Another "poem," or series of sonnets marked off by an editor as celebrating a particular time and its state of mind is Tucker Brooke's Group P, which he calls "St. Martin's Summer."[6] It includes seven sonnets, of which five are in the order of the 1609 Quarto; the other two have got misplaced. The seven sonnets preceding "St. Martin's Summer" need no reordering, in Brooke's view; they record an interruption in the relationship between the poet and the Fair Friend, or at least a hiatus in the celebration of it. But 104, the first "St. Martin's Summer" poem, starts afresh, with renewed vigor and eloquence: "To me, fair friend, you never can be old." This contradicts the admission in Sonnet 63, one of the Ovidian series, that the Fair Friend will age in time, just as the poet has done. Sonnet 104 then goes on to trace the career of the relationship with some specific detail. Three winters have shaken the summer's pride from the forests, three beauteous springs turned to yellow autumn, three April perfumes burned in three hot Junes. The triple insistence on the three-year endurance of the friendship has of course excited the biographical sleuths. There, at least, they argue, is something concrete to go on; we may not know when the relationship started but we know that it lasted three years. The biographical significance is weakened, however, when we realize that Horace's epode XI, 5-6, reads "The third December, since I

---

[6]*Shakespeare's Sonnets* (1936), pp. 190-96.

ceased to lust after Inachia, now is shaking the glory from the forests," and that Elizabethan schoolboys read Horace.[7]

However that may be, the celebration of renewed love runs through a comparison with idolatry (105), a comparison with the fairest wights described in old writings (106), the joyous survival of the friends' love (and the poet's verse) over a period when doom was prophesied by the makers of almanacs (107). It is succeeded by a comparison of the poet's verse to prayer (108); then, in Brooke's rearrangement, follow a comparison of love to a growing child (115) and a final definition of love as a permanent, ever-fixéd mark that looks on tempests and is never shaken. Brooke says this group "must be very nearly the greatest sonnets ever written."[8]

He does not, however, base this encomium on relationships between the sonnets but on magnificences within them. Usually the reordering of the sonnets is intended, one gathers, to promote credibility and plausibility of occasion rather more than to emphasize aesthetic excellence. Brooke does, indeed, have a theory about the mode of composition of the sonnets and the means of transmittal to the recipient. "We must guard against the notion that Shakespeare had at his service the penny post which would carry each sonnet to his friend as soon as it was composed, and against the opposite fallacy that he was planning for posterity a coherent sequence. The indications are that the sonnets were written most often in groups of two to five and dispatched to the recipient when opportunity served."[9]

The next important rearranger after Brooke was J. W. Lever in his book *The Elizabethan Love Sonnet* (1956). Lever attempted by reordering to make sense of the sonnets on the Fair Friend's fault; that these sonnets require rearrangement seemed to him indisputable:

The sonnets in which the Friend's sensuality is suspected but denied, admitted but excused, and finally accepted as one more contradiction in a bewildering universe, are spread through the main body of the collection from 33 to 96. There has certainly been disarrangement. The Poet, having said in 33 with reference to the Friend that "Suns of the world may stain" was not

[7]L. P. Wilkinson, "Shakespeare and Horace," *TLS* May 6, 1955, p. 237.
[8]*Op. cit.*, p. 73. For extreme praise of Sonnet 104, sometimes derided for its second line, "For as you were when first your eye I ey'd," see William Bowman Piper, "A Poem Turned in Process," *ELH* 43 (1976): 444–60.
[9]*Op. cit.*, p. 25.

likely to declare in 70 that the Friend presented a "pure unstained prime." Nor could he fairly claim in this latter sonnet that the Friend had "pass'd by the ambush of young days / Either not assail'd or victor being charg'd," after making the statement in 42: "That she hath thee is of my wailing chief." These anachronisms, which might pass in the theater, can hardly be disregarded in poems addressed to a reader, perhaps the Friend himself; and equally apparent is the incoherent succession of ideas and images in the Quarto order.[10]

In Lever's reading the series on the Friend's fault begins with Sonnet 67 ("Ah, wherefore with infection should he live") and its linked companion 68 ("Thus is his cheek the map of days outworn"). These two sonnets exhibit a characteristically Shakespearean revulsion against cosmetics and wigs. Sonnet 69 carries the condemnation further, suggesting that tongues praise the Friend's outward beauty but report an inward corruption. Sonnet 70 argues casuistically that the slander is undeserved:

> For canker vice the sweetest buds doth love,
> And thou present'st a pure unstainëd prime.
> Thou has pass'd by the ambush of young days,
> Either not assail'd, or victor being charg'd,
>
> (7–10)

This should be followed, Lever thought, by 95 and 96, which are clearly about the Friend's fault. In 95 the poet concedes that the Friend's beauty mitigates his vice but warns him against the abuse of "this large privilege." He then goes on to comment on how the Friend's grace and faults are so mixed that many might be seduced by them (96). Lever then continues with 94, which he quite rightly compares to a soliloquy in a play and says it clarifies the issues. The octave, about "They that have power to hurt and will do none" is, according to Lever, political, and derives from Sidney's *Arcadia*. The sestet or conclusion is of course moral.

Following this Lever puts the trio of sonnets 33–35, in which he says the effect of the fault upon the relationship between the Poet and the Fair Friend is explored. "The interplay of character adds a new factor, which in the course of three sonnets will appreciably modify the conclusions of 94."[11] The trio of sonnets compares the Fair Friend to the

---

[10] *The Elizabethan Love Sonnet* (1956), p. 209.
[11] *Ibid.*, p. 221.

sun, which appears early and promises a fair day, but then disappears behind the clouds (33, 34). The poet, however, manages to excuse the Friend for his fault and in so doing commits a fault himself:

> No more be griev'd at that which thou has done:
> Roses have thorns, and silver fountains mud,
> Clouds and eclipses stain both moon and sun,
> And loathsome canker lives in sweetest bud.
> All men make faults, and even I in this,
> Authorizing thy trespass with compare,
> Myself corrupting, salving thy amiss,
> Excusing [thy] sins more than [thy] sins are.

(35.1–8)[12]

A further suggestion of disarrangement is provided in the little series on rival poets, 78–86. These poems seem to belong together; they reflect various aspects of the poet's attitude toward other poets who seek the favor of the Fair Friend. The series leads up to extravagant praise of one or more of them in Sonnets 85–86.[13] Strangely at odds with its neighbors is Sonnet 81 ("Or I shall live your epitaph to make") which is a boast of the immortality of the speaker's verse. The subject was conventional, of course, and it is not necessary to suppose that 81 belongs with the other sonnets, such as 15, 18, 19, 55 and 60 which proclaim the permanence of verse. A poet may revert to a standard *topos* more than once, at different times and on different occasions, but to suppose that he would revert to it in the midst of sonnets which show uneasiness about his accomplishment in comparison with that of other poets is absurd.

There are various reasons for adopting the order of the 1609 Quarto (sometimes called Thorpe's order, though there is no evidence that

---

[12]Lever's sensitive critical comments are praised by L.C. Knights, *Some Shakespearean Themes*, pp. 164–66, but, as Knights points out, Lever has to over-read the sonnets in order to bring them together in a coherent pattern. Another objection to Lever's reordering is made by J.B. Leishman: "He perhaps too readily assumes that Shakespeare, like all other Elizabethan sonneteers, must necessarily have written them in a series of ordered sequences. He accordingly discusses them in groups, and this sometimes leads him to overlook the main theme of a sonnet because it does not happen to be that of the group in which he places it." *MLR* 52 (1957): 254.

[13]Muriel Bradbrook maintains in *Shakespeare the Craftsman*, pp. 31–32, that 85.2–4 describe a contest among poets at the Great Festival of the Pui, a guild of foreign merchants in London. I know of no evidence which would connect Shakespeare with such a festival.

Thorpe dictated the arrangement or numbered the sonnets). The first and most obvious is laziness. The second is skepticism about any of the arrangements that have so far been offered. This attitude is well expressed by Stephen Booth: "Although the sonnets invite scholarly rearrangements that fulfill the various kinds of continuity they signal, it is folly to accept the invitation."[14]

In 1949 Leslie Hotson, the most active and spectacular literary detective of the century, published a book called *Shakespeare's Sonnets Dated*, in which he tried to prove that Sonnet 107, with its reference to "the mortal moon," did not glance at Queen Elizabeth, but instead referred to the Spanish Armada, which according to some sources sailed in a crescent formation. This would mean an astonishingly early date for the sonnets, soon after 1588 and about a decade before they were referred to by Francis Meres. His argument provoked extensive controversy and was accepted by almost no scholars in the field. He returned to the charge in 1964 with *Mr. W. H.*, in which he nominated for the Fair Friend one William Hatliffe.

To bolster his argument for the connection between Sonnet 107 and the Armada, he made much of the psalms of thanksgiving which were part of the celebrations following the destruction of the Armada. He thought that Sonnets 107 and 124 refer to the psalms of the same numbers and that accordingly, "it will now be recognized that no one but their author could have given these last two sonnets the numbers 107 and 124. And if in the sequence these two stand correctly in their numbered places, it follows that the whole sequence 1 through 126 is correctly numbered: that the man who determined that order was therefore not Thomas Thorpe, nor anyone in the world but William Shakespeare." In a footnote he goes further and finds parallels in Sonnets 6, 32, 38, 53, and 102 with the corresponding psalms, which are the penetential psalms, favorite psalms for translation, paraphrase and commentary by those troubled with guilt or a sense of sin.[15]

The next contribution comes from one of the numerologists, Alastair Fowler, who constructs an elaborate scheme based on a triangular pattern. To make his mathematical game come out right he has to wrench the meaning of such lines as

---

[14]*Shakespeare's Sonnets* (1977), p. 546.
[15]*Mr. W. H.* (1964), pp. 280–81.

> Among a number one is reckon'd none.
> Then in the number let me pass untold. . . .
>
> (136.8–9)

He maintains that the sonnet is speaking, though line 14 clearly states that the speaker is a man named *Will.* After managing to subtract a few from the 154 in the Quarto, Fowler concludes: "The entire set of regular sonnets corresponds numerically to the entire set of psalms [150], though substantive correlations could only be communicated in the case of familiar psalms. Hotson's conclusion that Shakespeare numbered all of the sonnets himself is not yet proved, but we may fairly infer that he must have numbered a great many of them."[16]

Following this up, Kenneth Muir cites other parallels with the penitential psalms, and gracefully concedes, "Some of these parallels are obviously more significant than others, and some may well be fortuitous; but it is difficult not to believe that Shakespeare was aware of the links with the psalms. It is arguable, however, that at one state the links were closer than they are now. This is suggested by the fact that in several of the sonnets there are echoes of the adjacent psalms. The fountain, mentioned in Psalm 36, appears in Sonnet 35, the *idol* of Psalm 106 in Sonnet 105; and, more remotely, the lion of Psalm 17 appears two sonnets later, in No. 19."[17]

What would appear to be a weakness in the case for a correspondence between the psalms and the sonnets is here turned into an advantage: the former close correspondence has somehow been disturbed, establishing, if we believe it, another step in the formation of the text. But why should the psalms have anything to do with Shakespeare's sonnets anyway? The original reason seems to have been forgotten. Hotson wanted to relate the sonnets to thanksgiving for deliverance from the Armada, and many psalms (though certainly not the penitential ones) are songs of thanksgiving.

Rearrangers of the 1609 order have been most confident when dealing with the Dark Lady sonnets, 127–154. J. W. Mackail called them "a disordered appendix," a comment which has been repeated many times. It is extremely difficult, for instance, to justify the order of 144, 145, and 146. Of course 144 is the central sonnet of the Poet-Fair Friend-Dark Lady triangle:

---

16 *Triumphal Forms* (1970), p. 191.
17 "The Order of Shakespeare's Sonnets," *College Literature* 4 (1977): 195.

Two loves I have of comfort and despair,
Which like two spirits do suggest me still:
The better angel is a man right fair,
The worser spirit a woman color'd ill.

The following sonnet, 145, is sometimes called the worst in the whole collection. Apologists have supposed that it is early work, one critic going so far as to say that lines 13 and 14 refer, not to the Dark Lady at all, but to Anne Hathaway and must date from the poet's youth:

> "I hate" from hate away she threw,
> And sav'd my life, saying "not you."[18]

Number 146, the so-called "Christian" sonnet, is as far from this as one could imagine. In place of the frivolous or trivial play in 145 (with or without the supposed "hate away-Hathaway" pun) we have a sermon on the soul, the body, and death.

Michael J. B. Allen has undertaken to defend even this order. His essay is called "Shakespeare's Man Descending a Staircase,"[19] suggesting perhaps that the sonnets resemble the famous Cubist painting *Nude Descending a Staircase*, with its many overlapping planes. Allen sees the sonnets in groups of three, and any sonnet may occupy first, second, or third place in the group. Furthermore, for him there are dynamic relationships among the sonnets, which he likes to characterize with metaphors from physics: "144 has already activated images and themes and set up reverberations that do not bypass 145 so much as flow through it like microwaves"; "sonnet 146 does not merely give the lie to . . . sonnet 145 in order to validate the prayer that one may hate the sinful earth and the thrallèd heart, it also completes the circuit, whose negative pole is 144, and thus electrifies 145 and the attitudes attending it"; "just as the roles we adopt in life alternate perpetually between the progressive and the regressive, so these two sonnets pass through each other's fields of force."

Allen is in essence trying to justify the 1609 order: "I have been advocating alchemical ways, perhaps, for reading the sequence; but this is to reinforce, not undermine, the appropriateness of the Quarto's ordering . . . The Dark Lady sequence constitutes a painting in its

[18]Andrew Gurr, "Shakespeare's First Poem," *Essays in Criticism* 21 (1971): 221–26.
[19]*Shakespeare Survey* 31 (1978): 127–40.

own right and no justification exists for making it either more natural-
istic or more abstract . . . we should beware of critics who despair of
responding to the sonnets as they stand together." One sometimes
gets the feeling that critics of the Shakespeare sonnets come in a direct
line of descent from Tertullian, a Roman theologian who declared, "It
is certain because it is impossible."

II

Of the many absurdities in Shakespeare sonnet criticism, one of the
most persistent and long lived has been the chapter in Laura Riding
and Robert Grave's *A Survey of Modernist Poetry* in 1927.[20] It is an
attempt to justify the typographical novelties in the poetry of e e
cummings by a critical analysis of Shakespeare's Sonnet 129. Fifty years
after its publication Stephen Booth comments that "it is still often
treated with respect"[21] and devotes five pages to summarizing and discussing it. There are many minor mistakes in the Riding-Graves essay,
some of which Booth corrects, but the fundamental fallacy he
completely overlooks. The punctuation of the sonnet in the quarto of
1609 is not the work of the poet, but of one of two compositors in the
workshop of Eld, the printer. The characteristics of these two compositors have been carefully and accurately traced.[22]

When two compositors are thought to have worked on a quarto,
their stints can be distinguished from one another by variants in
spelling and punctuation. In both of these matters there was considerably more freedom in the Elizabethan printing house (and, for that
matter, in manuscript) than there is now. Here is a short table of
spelling preferences between Eld's two men, Compositor A and
Compositor B:

A	B
shalbe, wilbe	shall be, will be
ritch	rich
Oh	O
dost	doost, etc.

[20]In addition to the book, see Laura Riding, "Some Autobiographical Corrections
of Literary History," *University of Denver Quarterly* 8, No. 4 (1974): 1–33, especially
12–13.
[21]*Shakespeare's Sonnets* (1977), p. 447.
[22]MacD. P. Jackson, "Punctuation and the Compositors of Shakespeare's Sonnets,
1609," 5 *Library* 30 (1975): 1–24.

flowre, powre   flower, power
tongue   toung, etc.
                         ould, gould
                         noe, loe
                         -les, -nes

The two compositors differ also in punctuation, especially in their treatment of the third quatrain: "A ended it with a colon 10 times, a comma only once; B ended it with a colon 12 times, a comma 29 times." According to Jackson's count, B was the principal workman. He set forty-five of the sixty-five pages on which the sonnets are printed; compositor A set the other twenty. Jackson was able to form an opinion on the two compositors' respective skills: "Compositor A did not misread his copy stupidly, as B did. From the *Sonnets* I get the impression that A was the more intelligent person, but his susceptibility to memorial substitution may have caused more permanent damage to the text than B's dullness. A was, for example, responsible for the notorious crux in 146.2"[23] / the repeating of the last three words of line /, "my sinful earth," as the first three words of line 2.

Since we cannot actually see the copy Compositor B had in front of him, we must conjecture about it on the basis of our knowledge of his spelling and punctuation habits and the text he produced. The text of Sonnet 129 is reproduced here as it appears in the 1609 Quarto.

TH'expence of Spirit in a waste of shame
Is lust in action, and till action, lust
Is periurd, murdrous, blouddy full of blame,
Sauage, extreme, rude, cruell, not to trust,
Inioyd no sooner but dispised straight,
Past reason hunted, and no sooner had
Past reason hated as a swollowed bayt,
On purpose layd to make the taker mad.
Made In pursut and in possession so,
Had, hauing, and in quest, to haue extreame,
A blisse in proofe and proud and very wo,
Before a ioy proposed behind a dreame,
    All this the world well knowes yet none knowes well,
    To shun the heauen that leads men to this hell.

---

[23] *Op. cit.*, pp. 9–10.

126

> **129**
> TH'expence of Spirit in a waſte of ſhame
> Is luſt in action,and till action , luſt
> Is periurd,murdrous,bloudy full of blame,
> Sauage,extreame,rude,cruell,not to truſt,
> Inioyd no ſooner but diſpiſed ſtraight,
> Paſt reaſon hunted, and no ſooner had
> Paſt reaſon hated as a ſwollowed bayt,
> On purpoſe layd to make the taker mad.
> Made In purſut and in poſſeſſion ſo,
> Had,hauing,and in queſt,to haue extreame,
> A bliſſe in proofe and proud and very wo,
> Before a ioy propoſd behind a dreame,
>   All this the world well knowes yet none knowes well,
>   To ſhun the heauen that leads men to this hell.

What the modern editor must do first is to turn interior i into j where it stands for it, as in *periurd* in line 2 and *Inioyd* in line 5. Likewise with internal u where it represents v, as in *Sauage* in line 4 and, most importantly, *proud* in line 11. Immediately after this word B has repeated *and* instead of *a*. A conservative and intelligent editor will follow 1609 when it indicates pronunciation by spelling. A modern text which renders line 5

> Enjoyed no sooner but despised straight

does not indicate, as the Quarto does, that *inioyd* has two syllables and *despised* three. Modern spelling does not give adequate signal for the pronunciation of *swallowed* in line 7 (three syllables) or *possession* in line 9 (four syllables).[24] Most modern editors emend *Made* in line 9 to *Mad*,

---

[24]Compositor B is not helpful to an editor in the case of Sonnet 124, where the rhyming words of line 2 and line 4 are *vnfathered* and *gatherd*. The only other occurrence of the first of these words in the sonnets is in 97:

> Yet this aboundant issue seem'd to me
> But hope of Orphans, and vn-fathered fruit

but this is on a page set by Compositor A. In *Venus and Adonis*, which we know was set from Shakespeare's manuscript and was carefully printed, the word is spelled *gathred* (line 131).

though some defend the Quarto reading. Knowing that B very commonly closed the third quatrain with a comma where his colleague preferred a stronger punctuation, an editor should have no hesitation in changing it to a period.

From what we know of Shakespeare's own habits of punctuation in his part of the manuscript play *Sir Thomas More* we conclude that he punctuated very lightly and that most of the commas were inserted by B, who was quite prodigal with them. Therefore the insertion of a comma after *bloody* in line 3, after *had* in line 6, after *proof* and *proved* in line 11 are warranted liberties, as are the correction of the position of the comma in line 10 and its omission at the end of line 13.

Theodore Redpath, who has collaborated on an edition of the sonnets, is the author of an essay called "The Punctuation of Shakespeare's Sonnets."[25] He speculates on the practice in punctuating at Eld's printing shop without realizing that two compositors set up the quarto, wastes a good deal of space on Riding and Graves and on Percy Simpson's long-since discredited *Shakespearean Punctuation* (1911), and finally concludes that about 1,250 of the 2,155 lines in Shakespeare's *Sonnets* need repunctuating.

An instance of punctuation which seriously affects the meaning is that of the parentheses in line 11 of Sonnet 29, which the Quarto prints

> and then my state
> (Like to the Larke at breake of daye arising)
> From sullen earth sings himns at Haeuens gate,

causing difficulty to every succeeding editor. Simpson maintained that editors have no right to alter the punctuation of Q (mistakenly supposing that it was the poet's) but R. M. Alden replied, reasonably, that it seems safer to follow the maker of the simile than the printer of the parentheses. The situation is well summed up by Albert Howard Carter: "Conceivably we could end the parenthesis at 'daye,' at 'arising,' or at 'earth' in the following line. Or we can discard the parentheses altogether by understanding 'is' before 'Like' and a 'which' before 'sings.' Actually the poet's state becomes so completely merged with the lark to which he compares it that as elsewhere in Shakespeare it is not clear where one term of the metaphor begins and the other ends. And placing the parenthesis at any definite spot may do

---

[25] In Hilton Landry, ed., *New Essays on Shakespeare's Sonnets* (1976), pp. 217–51.

violence to one of the possible meanings since the identity of subject and thing compared contributes to the richness of the figure." [26]

We can see a good example of the work of Compositor A in Sonnet 94, which we examined early in this study as an example of a soliloquy sonnet. Its text in the 1609 Quarto is reproduced below.

94

THey that haue powre to hurt, and will doe none,
That doe not do the thing, they moſt do ſhowe,
Who mouing others, are themſelues as ſtone,
Vnmooued, could, and to temptation ſlow:
They rightly do inherrit heauens graces,
And husband natures ritches from expence,
They are the Lords and owners of their faces,
Others, but ſtewards of their excellence:
The ſommers flowre is to the ſommer ſweet,
Though to it ſelfe, it onely liue and die,
But if that flowre with baſe infeʧion meete,
The baſeſt weed out-braues his dignity:
    For ſweeteſt things turne ſowreſt by their deedes,
    Lillies that feſter, ſmell far worſe then weeds.

94

THey that haue powre to hurt, and will doe none,
That doe not do the thing, they most do showe,
Who mouing others, are themselues as stone,
Vnmooued, could, and to temptation slow:
They rightly do inherrit heauens graces,
And husband natures ritches from expence,
They are the Lords and owners of their faces,
Others, but stewards of their excellence:
The sommers flowre is to the sommer sweet,
Though to it selfe, it onely liue and die,
But if that flowre with base infection meete,
The basest weed out-braues his dignity:
    For sweetest things turne sowrest by their deedes,
    Lillies that fester, smell far worse then weeds.

---

[26] "The Punctuation of Shakespeare's Sonnets of 1609" in *Joseph Quincy Adams Memorial Studies* (1948), 409–28. The two compositors of the Quarto had not been identified when Carter wrote. He thought that there was "a system" to the punctuation but that the parentheses in 29 fell outside the system.

Here are some of A's characteristic spellings: *ritches* and *flowre*. Even more marked is his addiction to the colon as a punctuation mark. He uses it to close each of the quatrains, where B would probably have used commas. This heavy marking at the ends of lines 4, 8, and 12 has led some readers to see the structure as three quatrains and a couplet, even though the change in imagery, from heirs, property owners and stewards in the octave to flowers in the sestet gives the sonnet a two-part structure. The point is that the Quarto punctuation, not being Shakespeare's, is in no way a dependable guide to the structure or meaning of the sonnet.[27]

Sometimes readers who have consulted a facsimile of the Quarto of 1609 are curious about the use of italics. This matter becomes crucial to the interpretation of the notorious *Will* sonnets, particularly 135 and 136. It even shows up in the barnyard sonnet, 143, the couplet of which reads

> So will I pray that thou maist haue thy *Will*,
> If thou turn back and my loude crying still.

An amusing example of the ghost such a concern over italics can conjure up is the case of *Hews* in Sonnet 20.7: "A man in hew all *Hews* in his controwling." The idea occurred to Tyrwhitt, who passed it on to Edmond Malone, that the Fair Friend might be a man named Hughes. This created, in Hyder Rollins' words, "a spook harder to drive away than the ghost of Hamlet's father."[28] Malone's friend and editor, the younger Boswell, was skeptical because he noticed that other words like *Rose* (1.2), *Audit* (4.12), *Statues* (55.5), and *Autumne* (104.5) were also italicized. The prospectors were not discouraged, however, and they went on digging for a Will Hughes who was alive

---

[27] Carol Thomas Neely, in "Detachment and Engagement in Shakespeare's Sonnets," *PMLA* 92 (1977): 83–95, is strangely muddled about the punctuation of this sonnet. In note 11, page 93, she tries to defend her notion of the structure—three quatrains and a couplet—by saying "Modern editions help to create the division that modern critics discuss [i.e., octave and sestet thought structure] by their substitution of a period for Quarto's semicolon after 'excellence' and by (in many cases) removing Quarto's semicolon after 'slow'." In fact, there are no semicolons in the 1609 text of 94; they are colons, as even Neely's printing of the sonnet on p. 84 shows. The extent of her confusion is indicated in note 8, where she refers to "Folio's comma."

[28] Variorum *Sonnets*, 2: 181.

at the time the sonnets were written. Finally, Samuel Butler came up with a man of that name who was a sea cook.

What the prospectors failed to realize is that this habit of italicizing came from the compositors in Eld's printing house. Alice Walker noticed it when she was working on the text of *Troilus and Cressida*, the quarto of which was printed by Eld in 1609, the same year he printed the *Sonnets*. She commented: "A curious feature of the Quarto text which suggests that the MS. behind the text may have been intended for a reader or (more likely) used by a reader is its use of italics. Like most quartos it italicizes proper names in the dialogue, but it italicizes as well quite a number of fairly common words of learned origin: *maxim, chaos, indexes, modicums, pia mater, moral philosophy, quondam, major,* and also, very curiously, *Autumne* . . . They may, of course, be the compositor's, though the selection of words and phrases of this kind is unusual. . . ."[29]

Sonnet 16, set by Compositor B, offers some interesting problems in punctuation and interpretation. Its Quarto text reads:

> BVt wherefore do not you a mightier waie
> Make warre vppon this bloudie tirant time?
> And fortifie your selfe in your decay
> With meanes more blessed then my barren rime?
> Now stand you on the top of happie houres,
> And many maiden gardens yet vnset,
> With vertuous wish would beare your liuing flowers,
> Much liker then your painted counterfeit:
> So should the lines of life that life repaire
> Which this (Times pensel or my pupill pen)
> Neither in inward worth nor outward faire
> Can make you liue your selfe in eies of men,
>   To giue away your selfe, keeps your selfe still,
>   And you must liue drawne by your owne sweet skill.

The sonnet follows upon 15, which promises the Fair Friend renewal by the poet's verse as Time takes away his youthful beauty. But here the poet returns to the plea to the young man to marry and produce children, the "living flowers" of line 7, which will resemble

---

[29] "The Textual Problem of *Troilus and Cressida*," *MLR* 45 (1950): 461–62.

him more than his portrait. This conceit of the offspring in rivalry with "your painted counterfeit" dominates the sestet. The Fair Friend becomes, in line 14, the artist who paints a self-portrait. "The lines of life that life repair" is a way of saying, compactly, that hereditary lines create a kind of immortality by repairing the injury done by Time to the individual. To preserve the parentheses around "Time's pencil or my pupil pen" would lead the modern reader to suppose the words are in apposition to "this," which makes neither good sense nor good syntax. Removing the parentheses, however, makes "this time's pencil" mean something quite specific, like "the paint brush or engraving tool of this particular time," which is beginning to draw the lines of age in the fair face. (*Pencil* did not mean a writing instrument; *my pupil pen* means exactly that.) The richness of the imagery, from war to gardening to portraiture, leads to an epigrammatic couplet: to give away is to keep, and to live you must draw yourself with "your own sweet skill."

Modern editors have to make a decision about the two occurrences of *your self* in line 13; the compositor always separates them, but Ingram and Redpath print "To give away *yourself* keeps *your self* still" with the explanation: "We have retained Q in the second instance, so as to reflect a possible distinction between the bodily immortality referred to in line 12, and the perpetuation of the spiritual personality which may be referred to here."[30]

Ingram and Redpath also retain the parenthesis in line 10, although Tucker Brooke says, "The parenthesis in 16.10 makes no sense. Most likely the printer misread a perpendicular flourish of the capital 'T' in *Times* as an opening parenthesis mark, and closed the parenthesis on his own at the end of the line."[31]

The punctuation of Shakespeare's sonnets is, it seems, a circular process. The editor must first decide what the passage means, or what meanings he will allow for it, and then punctuate so that those meanings are available to the reader. In view of what is now known about the composition and printing of quartos in Eld's printing house in 1609, there is no justification for supposing that the punctuation in that quarto is Shakespeare's.[32]

---

[30]*Shakespeare's Sonnets* (1965), p. 40.

[31]*Shakespeare's Sonnets* (1936), pp. 60–61.

[32]MacD. P. Jackson thinks that features of the Quarto which cut across the compositorial divisions derive from the printer's manuscript copy. (5 *Library*

30[1975]: 13). He particularly finds that the distribution of internal commas does not differ by compositor but by position in the sequence, which he relates to date: "I am inclined to believe that the figures reflect difference between groups of sonnets of differing metrical and syntactical complexity." I think this is stretching the evidence beyond the breaking point. The groups he refers to are arbitrary blocks of 25 sonnets each. We know from Hand D in *Sir Thomas More* that Shakespeare punctuated very lightly. See *The Riverside Shakespeare*, ed. G. B. Evans *et al.*, p. 1,684 b.

CHAPTER SIX

Some Readers of the Sonnets

Not the least interesting aspect of the sonnets is the way they have been read. Awareness of their poetic value has varied with the vogue of the sonnet as a verse form, with critical doctrines about the virtues of the Italian versus the English structure, and with prevailing attitudes toward the expression of love between members of the same sex. There are linguistic readings, rhetorical readings, philosophic readings, to say nothing of the many mystery-story readings. Sometimes the comments of gifted and sensitive readers are tantalizingly brief, for example that of Keats:

> One of the three books I have with me is Shakespear's Poems: I never found so many beauties in the sonnets—they seem to be full of fine things said unintentionally—in the intensity of working out conceits—Is this to be borne? Hark ye!
>
> > When lofty trees I see barren of leaves
> > Which erst from heat did canopy the herd
> > And summer's green all girded up in sheaves
> > Borne on the bier with white and bristly beard.[1]

Keats used lines 11–12 of Sonnet 17 as an epigraph for *Endymion*:

> > And your true rights be term'd a poet's rage
> > And stretchëd metre of an antique song.

He also quoted 19.10 ("Nor draw no lines there with thine antique pen"), 21.7 ("With April's first-born flowers, and all things rare"), and 13.2 ("No longer yours than you yourself here live").

I offer only a sample of readers far less attuned to the Shakespeare of the sonnets than was John Keats. I realize that some of them may be more entertaining than enlightening.

---

[1] *The Letters of John Keats*, ed. Hyder E. Rollins, 1: 188–89.

If the persons addressed in the sonnets are actual rather than imaginary, and if they were presented with the sonnets addressed to them, they are the first readers of whom we have any knowledge: the young bachelor in Sonnets 1–17, the Fair Friend (if he is different from the young bachelor) who is the main subject of Sonnets 18–125, and the Dark Lady, who is sometimes described (138 "When my love swears that she is made of truth") and sometimes addressed (141 "In faith, I do not love thee with mine eyes"). After that, we next have a somewhat cryptic reference to the "private friends" who had manuscript copies of some "sugared sonnets," according to Francis Meres in 1598.[2]

In the next year, readers of *The Passionate Pilgrim*, an odd little miscellany of love poems, could read five sonnets by Shakespeare, three from *Love's Labor's Lost* and two sonnets central to the Dark Lady group, numbers 138 and 144 ("Two loves I have, of comfort and despair"). They are the first two items in the miscellany.

These are the only indications we have of readers of Shakespeare's sonnets before the publication of the whole lot of them in Thomas Thorpe's quarto of 1609. Though some have supposed that the edition of that year was suppressed, there is no real reason to think so. Thirteen copies have survived. The sonnet craze died down at the end of the sixteenth century (though Daniel and Drayton continued to republish, revise, and supplement their cycles). Religious sonnets continued to be written, but love sonnets were passé.

In the second decade of the seventeenth century we have a piece of evidence, recently discovered, showing that some readers valued Shakespeare's sonnets very highly. A book of sonnets by Lope de Vega, published in 1613, survives at Oxford. It has on the fly-leaf a note by Leonard Digges, then in Spain, to a friend at Oxford:

> Will Baker: Knowinge
> That Mr Mab: was to
> sende you this Booke
> of sonnets wch with Spaniards
> here is accounted of their
> lope de Vega as in Englande
> wee sholde of or: Will
> Shakespeare. I colde not

---

[2] *Francis Mere's Treatise "Poetrie,"* ed. Don Cameron Allen (1933), p. 76.

but insert thus much to
you, that if you like
him not, you must neuer
neuer reade Spanishe poet   LEO: Digges[3]

Leonard Digges (1588–1635) was the stepson of the man Shakespeare chose to be the overseer of his will. Additional evidence that Digges knew the sonnets may be found in the short poem by him in the First Folio, just after the table of contents. It has often been observed that Digges refers to the Stratford monument, but not that he seems to have the sonnets in mind:

> This Booke,
> When Brasse and Marble fade, shall make thee looke
> Fresh to all Ages; when Posteritie
> Shall loath what's new, think all is prodegie
> That is not Shake-speares; eu'ry Line, each Verse
> Here shall revive, redeeme thee from thy Herse,
> Nor fire, nor cankring Age, as Naso said,
> Of his, they wit-fraught Booke shall once inuade.

The idea is commonplace in Ovid and Horace, but the language Digges uses is that of Shakespeare's sonnets.

Digges' longer tribute, focused on the originality of the plays and actively opposing Ben Jonson, was not published until 1640, in Benson's edition of the "Poems," but John Freehafer has shown that it was written sometime in the period 1630–34. He also makes it seem very likely that the verses were written in opposition to Jonson's eulogy and were intended for publication in the Second Folio. They did not appear in that volume, but they may have remained in the printing house of Thomas Cotes, who printed the Second Folio in 1632 and Benson's edition of the "Poems" in 1640.

Sir John Suckling was born in 1609, the year Shakespeare's sonnets were published. The gossip-biographer John Aubrey says of him that after his travels he returned to England

---

[3]Paul Morgan, "Our Will Shakespeare and Lope de Vega: An Unrecorded Document," *Shakespeare Survey* 16 (1963): 118 ff. Digges and his contributions are discussed in John Freehaver, "Leonard Digges, Ben Jonson, and the Beginning of Shakespeare Idolatry," *Shakespeare Quarterly* 21 (1970): 63–75.

an extraordinary accomplished Gent., grew famous at Court for his readie sparkling wit; which was envyed, and he was (Sir William Davenant sayd) the Bull that was bayted. He was incomparably readie at repartyng, and his Witt most sparkling when most sett-upon and provoked. He was the greatest gallant of his time, and the greatest Gamester. . . . He was one of the best Bowlers of his time in England. He played at Cards rarely well, and did use to practise by himselfe a-bed, and there studyed how the best way of managing the cards could be . . . Sir William Davenant (who was his intimate friend and loved him intirely) would say that Sir John, when he was at his lowest ebbe in gameing, I mean when unfortunate, then would make himselfe most glorious in apparell, and sayd it exalted his spirits, and that he had then best Luck when he was most gallant, and his Spirits were highest.[4]

He is known today as the quintessential cavalier poet, the author of "Why so pale and wan, fond lover?" and

> Out upon it! I have loved
>   Three whole days together;
> And am like to love three more
>   If it prove fair weather.

He also wrote some plays, now known only to scholars. That he was an admirer of Shakespeare and kept company with others who were is suggested by an anecdote in Nicholas Rowe's Life of Shakespeare prefixed to his edition of the *Works* in 1709:

"In a conversation between Sir *John Suckling*, Sir *William Davenant*, *Endymion Porter*, Mr. *Hales* of Eaton, and *Ben Johnson*; Sir *John Suckling*, who was a profess'd admirer of *Shakespear*, had undertaken his Defence with some warmth; Mr. *Hales*, who had sat still for some time, hearing *Ben* frequently reproaching him with the want of Learning, and Ignorance of the Antients, told him at last, *That if* Mr. Shakespear *had not read the Antients, He had likewise not stollen anything from 'em*; (a Fault the other made no Conscience of) *and that if he would produce any one Topick finely treated by any of them, he would undertake to shew something upon the same Subject at least as well written by* Shakespear."[5]

Confirming evidence of Suckling's admiration for the playwright is provided in his portrait by Van Dyck, now in the Frick Collection in

[4]*Aubrey's Brief Lives*, ed. Oliver Lawson Dick (1950), pp. 287–88.
[5]I: xiv.

New York City. The subject chose to be painted holding a folio Shakespeare open at *Hamlet*.[6]

His admiration extended to the sonnets. In his play *Brennoralt, A Tragedy*, written about 1640, he borrows from six of them, and echoes two others. Shakespeare's Sonnet 9 has the lines

> Look what an unthrift in the world doth spend
> Shifts but his place, for still the world enjoys it.
>
> (9.9–10)

Suckling makes this

> How like an unthrift's case will mine be now?
> For all the wealth he looses shifts but's place
> And still the world enjoys it.[7]

Sonnet 47 has the conceit

> When that mine eye is famish'd for a look,
> Or heart in love with sighs himself doth smother,
> With my love's picture then my eye doth feast,
> And to the painted banquet bids my heart.

Suckling makes this into a plea from Iphigene to Francelia:

> Will you not send me neither
> Your picture when y'are gone?
> That, when my eye is famisht for a looke
> It may have where to feed,
> And to the painted feast invite my heart.[8]

Another conceit attracts him in Sonnet 104:

> Ah, yet doth beauty, like a dial hand,
> Steal from his figure, and no pace perceiv'd
>
> (104. 9–10)

In *Brennoralt* it is spoken at a dramatic moment, the death of Francelia:

> She's gone!
> Life, like a dial's hand hath stolne
> From the fair figure, ere it was perceiv'd.[9]

---

[6] *The Works of Sir John Suckling: The Plays*, ed. L. A. Beaurline (1971), p. vii.
[7] *Ibid.*, p. 231.
[8] *Ibid.*, p. 227.
[9] *Ibid.*, p. 231.

In an earlier passage in the play Suckling combines fragments from three different sonnets:

> So am I as the rich whose blessed key
> Can bring him to his sweet-uplockëd treasure,
> The which he will not ev'ry hour survey,
> For blunting the fine point of seldom pleasure.   (52. 1–4)
>
> Thou that art now the world's fresh ornament   (1.9)
>
> That thou among the wastes of time must go.   (12.10)

Suckling fuses these into a soliloquy by Brennoralt when he sees Francelia asleep:

> So misers look upon their gold, which while
> They joy to see, they fear to lose; The pleasure
> Of the sight scarse equalling the jealousie
> Of being dispossesst by others . . .
> Heavens! shall this fresh ornament of the world,
> This precious loveliness pass with other common things
> Among the wastes of time, what pity 'twere.[10]

It is evident that Suckling's mind was saturated with Shakespeare's sonnets when he wrote *Brennoralt*, about 1640.

In that exact year, twenty-four years after Shakespeare's death, a publisher, John Benson, whose principal interests were in the works of Ben Jonson and his school, decided to publish an edition of Shakespeare's poems. He did not have the rights to *Venus and Adonis* and *Lucrece*; they had been published as recently as 1638 and 1632, respectively, by others who held the rights. But the rights to the *Sonnets* of 1609 had lapsed, or rather reverted to the Stationers' Company when Thomas Thorpe went out of business. *The Passionate Pilgrim* had never been entered by the fraudulent William Jaggard, who published three editions of it. (He was forced to remove Shakespeare's name from the third edition in 1612, in which he had inserted some poems by Thomas Heywood.) Benson entrusted the printing to Thomas Cotes, who had printed the Second Folio of Shakespeare's plays in 1632.

---

[10]*Ibid.*, p. 216.

The accounts given of Benson and his project are usually misleading. Hyder Rollins, in his great Variorum edition of the sonnets, denounces him roundly as a pirate and accordingly dismisses his edition as of no value. Indeed, because Benson combined, reordered and titled the "Poems," and in a few instances changed pronouns to indicate that the verses were addressed to a woman instead of a man, Benson's text has been held by some to have negative value, less than no value at all.

I shall treat Benson as a reader of the sonnets. He obviously had before him a copy of the 1609 Quarto and the 1612 edition of *The Passionate Pilgrim* with Shakespeare's name on the title page. He composed a prose preface "To the Reader" and included an engraving of Shakespeare by William Marshall. He included the longer poem by Leonard Digges already discussed and a short poem by one John Warren praising "these learned poems."

Benson's preface was composed in a peculiar way. He assured readers of the poems that

In your perusall you shall finde them Seren, cleare, and eligantly plaine, such gentle straines as shall recreate and not perplexe your braine, no intricate or cloudy stuffe to puzzell intellect, but perfect eloquence. . . ."

Such language seems very odd applied to Shakespeare's sonnets, which may be serene but can hardly be called clear and elegantly plain. They have perplexed the brains of many, and their latest editor has found sufficient intricate and cloudy stuff to puzzle intellect to justify his elaborate analytical commentary.

The explanation is one that I found thirty years ago: Benson was merely rephrasing a poem he had published five years earlier—a commendatory poem by Thomay May, a Ben Jonson disciple, in praise of Joseph Rutter, another member of the tribe of Ben, on his pastoral tragicomedy, *The Shepheards Holy-Day.*[11] So Benson was economical, and of course commercial. He was writing a blurb and to save himself trouble he simply went back to one of his previous publications and rephrased it.

The old charge that he was a pirate has been discredited, most

---

[11]"'No Cloudy Stuffe to Puzzell Intellect': A Testimonial Misapplied to Shakespeare," *Shakespeare Quarterly* 1 (1950): 18–21.

recently by Josephine Waters Bennett.[12] Following Shakespeare's "Poems," i. e., the sonnets and the contents of *The Passionate Pilgrim*, are three elegies on Shakespeare by I. M. (John Milton), W. B. (William Basse), and an anonymous author, all taken from the Second Folio of 1632. After this there is a group called *An Addition of some Excellent Poems, to these precedent, of Renowned Shakespeare, By other Gentlemen*. Benson entered this in the Stationers' Register and paid his fee for it. This is not the action of a pirate. Mrs. Bennett's conclusion is definitive: "Benson no doubt hoped to make a little money on this volume, but he took considerable pains with it, not only by the elaborate (if mistaken) rearrangement of the neglected volumes of lyrics, but by the additions. . . . The *Poems* of 1640 is not a pirated edition of *Shake-speares Sonnets* but an edition to rescue them from oblivion, as it did."[13]

Eight sonnets of the 1609 collection (18, 19, 43, 56, 75, 76, 96, and 126) are missing in Benson's *Poems*. It is not easy to discover why.[14] The omissions include two of the great sonnets, 18 ("Shall I compare thee to a summer's day?") and 19 ("Devouring Time, blunt thou the lion's paws"), but the others are not so valuable. Number 126 ("O thou, my lovely boy") may have been omitted because it is a 12-line poem in couplets, but it is also possible that moral reasons were behind the exclusion. Benson changed *him* to *her* in 101.11 and 14 and changed *sweet boy* to *sweet love* in 108.5. Sometimes the titles Benson supplied identify the person addressed as a woman where the sonnet itself gives no clear indication: Sonnet 113 ("Since I left you, mine eye is in my mind") is titled *Selfe flattery of her beautie*; Sonnet 122 is titled *Vpon the receit of a Table Booke from his Mistris*; Sonnet 125 ("Were't aught to me I bore the canopy") is titled *An intreatie for her acceptance*. Though the titles seem jejune to those who know the sonnets well, we should

---

[12] Josephine Waters Bennett, "Benson's Alleged Piracy of *Shake-speares Sonnets* and some of Jonson's Works," *Studies in Bibliography* 21 (1968): 235–48.

[13] *Ibid.*, p. 248. Further discussion was carried on in the correspondence columns of the *Times Literary Supplement* on May 3, 10, 17, and 24, 1974. The final contribution, by Peter Grant, substantiates the Bennett case.

[14] Raymond Macdonald Alden, who demonstrated that the 1609 Quarto, and not manuscript, was the source of Benson's 1640 *Poems*, remarked, "I am not without hope that some reader of this paper will be more fortunate than I in explaining just what happened to cause the loss of the sonnets which did not reappear in 1640." *M. P.* 14 (1916–17): 30. Bennett suggests that Benson thought 96 and 126 defective, and that the other six "could have been simply missed" (op. cit., p. 236, n.6).

remember that titles of this sort go back as far as the first of the great collections of poetry, Tottel's Miscellany (1557). In that book Surrey's sonnet "Set me whereas the sun doth parch the green" is titled *Vow to love faithfully however he be rewarded.* Wyatt's sonnet "The long love that in my heart doth harbor" is called *The Lover for Shame- fastness Hideth his Desire within his Faithful Heart.* Nor did the fashion stop in mid-century. The very popular *England's Helicon* (1600, 1614) helps out the reader of the beautiful lyric "Come away, come, sweet love" by supplying the title *To his Love.* Inasmuch as he combined the sonnets into "poems," Benson's practice of supplying titles was normal for the period.

There are two possible reasons for Benson's combining the sonnets into "Poems." The first is that sonnets of the traditional Elizabethan sort, separate poems of fourteen lines each, were not popular in 1640. Furthermore, Benson was aware of links between the sonnets, links that sometimes bind as many as five sonnets together. For example, he makes 8, 9, 10, 11, and 12 into one poem under the title "An Invitation to Marriage." Sonnets 60, 63, 64, 65, and 66 are combined under the title "Injurious Time." He saw 61 ("Is it thy will thy image should keep open") and 62 ("Sin of self-love possesseth all mine eye") as not belonging to the series on time; instead he inserted them separately with rather cryptic Latin titles, *Patiens Armatus* and *Sat fuisse* respectively. He brought together 127, 130, 131, and 132 under the title *In prayse of her beautie though black*; 128 ("How oft when thou, my music, music play'st") appears separately as *Upon her playing on the Virginals*, and 129 ("Th'expense of spirit in a waste of shame") under the obvious title *Immoderate Lust.*

Apparently Benson thought *The Passionate Pilgrim* carried equal or superior authority to the 1609 Quarto of the sonnets, because he printed 138 and 144 from the *Pilgrim*, and did not repeat them when he came to them in the 1609 text. He scooped up the first three items of the *Pilgrim* just after his selection of five sonnets inviting to marriage; then he returned to the 1609 quarto but could find no linkage in 21, 22, 23, so he gave each a title. Number 21 ("So is it not with me as with that Muse") is called *True Content*, presumably because of its couplet:

> Let them say more that like of hearsay well,
> I will not praise that purpose not to sell.

Twenty-three ("As an unperfect actor on the stage") is called *A bashful Lover*. Sonnet 22 ("My glass shall not persuade me I am old") is a complicated poem, with shifting imagery and a paradoxical couplet:

> Presume not on thy heart when mine is slain,
> Thou gav'st me thine not to give back again.

Benson apparently did not find it as serene, clear and elegantly plain as he did some others, so he called it *Strong conceite*. He liked titles consisting of an adjective and a noun: *Quicke prevention, Youthfull glory, True content, Immoderate Passion*. In general, it seems Benson read the sonnets with concern for the topics they treat, the more standard the better. He was what Richard L. Levin would call a "thematic reader,"[15] but his motivation was clearly commercial and he may well have thought that the taste which had made poetical miscellanies popular forty years before was still exploitable.

Apparently there were few readers of the sonnets in their original form for more than a century, and when we look for one in the late eighteenth century we encounter the remarkable George Steevens, one of the great Shakespeare editors of the age, along with Johnson, Capell, and Malone, the greatest of all. But with respect to the sonnets, Steevens was not so much a non-reader as an anti-reader. His hyperbolic condemnation of the sonnets is famous and has not been surpassed:

We have not reprinted the Sonnets, &c. of Shakespeare, because the strongest act of Parliament that could be framed, would not compel readers into their service; notwithstanding these miscellaneous poems have derived every possible advantage from the literature and judgement of their only intelligent editor, Mr. Malone, whose implements of criticism, like the ivory rake and golden spade in Prudentius, are on this occasion disgraced by the objects of their culture. . . . Had Shakespeare produced no other works than these, his name would have reached us with as little celebrity as time has conferred on Thomas Watson, an elder and much more elegant sonneteer.[16]

Steevens' failure to respond to the poetic qualities in Shakespeare's sonnets is hardly comprehensible. No doubt, like Samuel Johnson, he disliked metaphysical conceits and wordplay, but he was not blind and

---

[15] *New Readings vs. Old Plays* (1979).
[16] "Advertisement" to the 1793 edition of the *Plays*, I: vii–viii.

deaf to poetry. He responded to the style of his own time. Valentine's soliloquy at the beginning of V, iv in *Two Gentlemen of Verona* offers an example:

> How use doth breed a habit in a man!
> This shadowy desert, unfrequented woods,
> I better brook than flourishing peopled towns:
> Here can I sit alone, unseen of any,
> And to the nightingale's complaining notes
> Tune my distresses and record my woes.
> O thou that dost inhabit in my breast,
> Leave not the mansion so long tenantless,
> Lest growing ruinous, the building fall
> And leave no memory of what it was!
> Repair me with thy presence, Sylvia;
> Thou gentle nymph, cherish thy forlorn swain.

Steevens has nothing to say about the first six lines; their pastoral nostalgia might please a modern reader and perhaps an Elizabethan playgoer too. But what the eighteenth-century critic liked was the four lines 7–10. Steevens comments, "It is hardly possible to point out four lines, in any of the plays of Shakespeare, more remarkable for ease and elegance."

Steevens was cantankerous and perverse. It was said of him by a contemporary that he had only three friends, and one of them was himself. When he found it necessary to explicate some bawdy language in Shakespeare, he attributed the indecent commentary to two respectable clergymen who had incurred his displeasure.

Despite his pronouncement in 1793 that nobody could be forced to read the sonnets, he had himself reprinted them in 1766 in his *Twenty of the Plays of Shakespeare*. He offered no commentary or explanation of the sonnets when he reprinted them, however; he may have been put off by the elaborate commentaries on Petrarch:

An hundred strappadoes, according to an Italian comick writer, would not have induced Petrarch, were he living, to subscribe to the meaning which certain commentators after his death have by their glosses extorted from his works.

Though he would not bother to comment on the sonnets in his own edition of them, he was willing to assist Edmond Malone when he prepared his Supplement of 1780. Malone printed Steevens' comments, even when he disagreed with them, and added his own. The dialogue sometimes reveals the personalities of the two men. An example is their comment on the couplet of Sonnet 1: "Pity the world, or else this glutton be / To eat the world's due, by the grave and thee." "The ancient editors of Shakespeare's works," wrote Steevens,

deserve at least the praise of impartiality. If they have occasionally corrupted his noblest sentiments, they have likewise depraved his most miserable conceits; as perhaps, in this instance. I read (piteous constraint, to read such stuff at all)

> —this glutton be
> To eat the world's due, *be thy* grave and thee.

. . . I did not think the late Mr. Rich had such example for the contrivance of making Harlequin jump down his own throat.[17]

To this sour comment Malone replied,

I do not think there is any corruption in the text . . . Our author's plays, as well as the poems now before us, affording a sufficient number of conceits, it is rather hard that he should be answerable for such as can only be obtained through the medium of alteration.

Steevens was not always quietly ironic. Sonnet 20 ("A woman's face with Nature's own hand painted") drove him into a rage: "It is impossible to read this fulsome panegyrick, addressed to a male object, without an equal measure of disgust and indignation."[18]

Steevens thought Sonnet 23 ("As an unperfect actor on the stage") derived from young Shakespeare's seeing traveling players at Stratford. This led Malone to make one of his most interesting and characteristic comments:

The *seeing* a few plays exhibited by a company of strollers in a barn at Stratford, or in Warwick Castle, would not however have made Shakespeare acquainted with the *feelings* of a timid actor on the stage. It has never been

---

[17]*Supplement* I: 582. John Rich (1682?-1761) known now chiefly as the producer of Gay's *Beggar's Opera*, was famous in his own time as an actor called Lun who played Harlequin. He figures in Pope's *Dunciad* III, 261 ff.
[18]*Supplement* I: 596.

supposed that our author was himself a player before he came to London. Whether the lines before us were founded on experience, or observation, cannot be ascertained. What I have advanced is merely conjectural.

When confronted with the sonorous beauty of Sonnet 30 ("When to the sessions of sweet silent thought") Steevens fretted at his inability to turn it into clear, understandable prose:

Such laboured perplexities of language, and such studied deformities of style, prevail throughout these sonnets, that the reader (after our best endeavours at explanation) will frequently find reason to exclaim with Imogen

> 'I see before me, man; nor here [nor] here,
> Nor what ensues, but have a fog in them
> That I cannot look through!'[19]

Complaints about Shakespeare's wordiness, which can be found as early as Thomas Rymer in the seventeenth century and as late as Matthew Arnold in the nineteenth, are unsurprisingly found in Steevens. His comment on 51, the second of two sonnets on the poet's traveling of horseback away from the Fair Friend, is an exclamation: "Such a profusion of words, and only to tell us that our author's passion was impetuous, though his horse was slow!"[20]

Shakespeare is attacked for botanical inaccuracy in "The canker-blooms have full as deep a dye / As the perfumèd tincture of the roses" (54.5-6). In Steevens' view, "Shakespeare had not yet begun to observe the productions of nature with accuracy, or his eyes would have convinced him that the *cynorhodon* is by no means as deep a colour as the *rose*, but what has truth or nature to do with Sonnets?" The question answers itself, but one regrets that chronology made it impossible for Steevens to comment on Keat's identification of Cortez as the discoverer of the Pacific Ocean.

Steevens was a watchdog over logic as well as botany. When he encountered the first two lines of Sonnet 63: "Against my love shall be as I am now / With Time's injurious hand crush'd and o'erworn," he sneered, "To say that a thing is first *crush'd*, and then *over-worn*, is little

---

[19]*Ibid.*, 606. The quotation is from *Cymbeline* III, ii, 78-80.
[20]*Supplement* I: 622.

better than to observe of a man, that he was first *killed*, and then *wounded*."[21]

Despite his scorn of the sonnet form and his dogged pursuit of logic, Steevens was not insensitive to poetic imagery. His comment on the first quatrain of Sonnet 73 is refreshing:

> That time of year thou mayst in me behold
> When yellow leaves, or none, or few, do hang
> Upon those boughs which shake against the cold,
> Bare [ruin'd] choirs, where late the sweet birds sang.

"This image," wrote Steevens,

> was probably suggested to Shakespeare by our desolated monasteries. The resemblance between the vaulting of a Gothic isle [sic] and an avenue of trees whose upper branches meet and form an arch over-head, is too striking not to be acknowledged. When the roof of the one is shattered, and the boughs of the other leafless, the comparison becomes more solemn and picturesque.

A spirited debate with Malone on the relation between poetry and life was instigated by the notion of Oldys (not rejected by Malone) that Sonnet 93 reflects Shakespeare's jealousy of his own wife:

> So shall I live, supposing thou art true,
> Like a deceivèd husband. . . .

Steevens here, like his former collaborator Samuel Johnson, is willing to lay down a general rule: "No argument, in my opinion, is more fallacious than that which imputes the success of a poet to his interest in his subject. Accuracy of description can be expected only from a mind at rest. It is the unruffled lake that is a faithful mirror." But Malone was too skillful a debater to be caught by such a trick. He replied, "I must still think that a poet's intimate knowledge of the passions and manners which he describes, will generally be of use to him; and that in some *few* cases experience will give a warmth to his colouring, that mere observation may not supply. No man, I believe, who has not felt the power of beauty, ever composed love-verses that were worth reading . . . That in order to produce any successful

---

[21]*Ibid.*, I. 657.

composition, the mind must be at ease, is, I conceive, an incontro-
vertible truth. I never supposed that Shakespeare wrote on the subject
of jealousy during the paroxysm of the fit."

Much of Steevens' animosity is toward the sonnet form itself. He
invokes the legendary Procrustes, as Ben Jonson and Stefano Guazzo
had done before him:[22]

A Sonnet was surely the contrivance of some literary Procrustes. The single
thought of which it is to consist, however luxuriant, must be cramped
within fourteen verses, or, however scanty, must be spun out into the same
number. On a chain of certain links the existence of metrical whim depends;
and its reception is secure as soon as the admirers of it have counted their
expected and statutable proportion of rhimes. The gratification of head or
heart, is no object of the writer's ambition. That a few of these trifles
deserving a better character may be found, I shall not venture to deny; for
chance co-operating with art and genius, will occasionally produce
wonders."[23]

Even this small concession, that possibly *some* sonnets are excellent
poetry, did not qualify Steevens' conclusion about the form: "Perhaps,
indeed, quaintness, obscurity and tautology are to be regarded as the
constituent parts of this exotick species of composition. But, in
whatever the excellence of it may consist, I profess I am one of those
who should have wished it to expire in the country where it was
born."

To this contention Malone offered something between the Retort
Courteous and the Quip Modest. He was probably no more liberated
from neoclassic doctrine than Steevens was, but he was devoted to
Shakespeare and he believed in moderation:

I do not feel any great propensity to stand forth as the champion of these
compositions. However, as it appears to me that they have been somewhat
under-rated, I think it incumbent on me to do them justice to which they are
entitled . . . When they are described as a mass of affectation, pedantry,
circumlocution, and nonsense, the picture appears to me overcharged. Their
great defects seem to be a want of variety, and the majority of them not

[22]R. F. Patterson, *Ben Jonson's Conversations with Drummond of Harthornden* (1923),
pp. 6-7.
[23]*Supplement* I: 682.

being directed to a female, to whom alone ardent expressions of esteem could with propriety be addressed. It cannot be denied too that they contain some far-fetched conceits; but are our author's plays entirely free from them? . . . I do not perceive the versification of these pieces is less smooth and harmonious than that of Shakespeare's other compositions. Though many of them

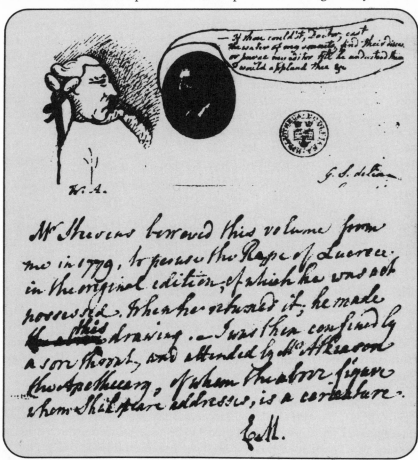

A caricature by George Steevens in Edmond Malone's copy of *The Rape of Lucrece* (1594). The sketch pictures Shakespeare addressing the apothecary Atkinson, who was attending Malone for a sore throat. He says "If thou could'st, Doctor, cast the water of my sonnets, find their disease, or purge my editor till he understood them I would applaud thee &c." See *Macbeth* V, iii, 50–53. The larger handwriting is Malone's. Reprinted with the permission of the Bodleian Library.

are not so simple and clear as they ought to be, yet some of them are written with perspicacity and energy. A few have already been pointed out as deserving this character; and many beautiful lines, scattered through these poems, will, it is supposed, strike every reader who is not determined to allow no praise to any species of poetry except blank verse and heroic couplets.[24]

James Boswell the Younger, who knew both of them, gives this account of the two men:

Mr. Steevens having published a second edition of his Shakespeare, in 1778, Mr. Malone, in 1780, added two supplementary volumes, which contained some additional notes, Shakespeare's poems, and seven plays which have been ascribed to him. There appears up to this time to have been no interruption to their friendship, but, on the contrary, Mr. Steevens, having formed a design of relinquishing all future editorial labours, most liberally made a present to Mr. Malone of his valuable collection of old plays, declaring that he himself was now become "a dowager commentator."[25]

The interruption in their friendship came when, in 1783, Malone argued against some of Steevens' explanations of passages in Shakespeare. Steevens demanded that Malone repeat these arguments in his next edition, together with Steevens' refutations of them. Malone declined and republished with revisions in 1790, whereupon Steevens declared that all communication on Shakespeare was over between them.

Boswell continued, of course, to preserve their contributions to Shakespeare scholarship; they form the greatest part of the great Variorum of 1821, the most compendious edition for a century and still not completely obsolete. His summary judgment of the two men is valuable:

Mr. Steevens was in many respects peculiarly qualified for the duties of an editor. With great diligence, an extensive acquaintance with early English literature, and a remarkably retentive memory; he was, as Mr. Gifford has justly observed, "a wit and a scholar." But his wit, and the sprightliness of his style, were too often employed to bewilder and mislead us. His consciousness of his own satirical powers made him much too fond of

---

[24]*Ibid.* 1: 684-85.
[25]*A Biographical Memoir of the Late Edmond Malone, Esq.* (1814), p. 8.

exercising them at the expense of truth and justice. . . . If Mr. Malone had
not the pointed vivacity of Mr. Steevens' manner (although his style was
remarkable for its elegance, perspicuity, and precision) yet he was equal in
critical sagacity, and superior even to him in accurate knowledge and
unwearied research; but he was still more honourably distinguished by his
openness of character and inflexible adherence to truth, from which he never
was withdrawn, either by a wish to support an hypothesis or to vex a rival.[26]

At the opposite extreme from George Steevens is George Wyndham
(1863–1913), a century later. If Steevens illustrates the limitations of the
neoclassic attitude and the personal oddities of a waspish, disdainful,
solitary scholar, George Wyndham illustrates the limitations of the
dedicated romantic and the personal qualities of a loveable, gracious,
versatile Englishman, perhaps the closest counterpart his time could
offer to Sir Philip Sidney. Like Sidney, a scion of an aristocratic family,
a soldier, poet, and critic, Wyndham was in addition a statesman. Sir
Shane Leslie wrote of him, "When George Wyndham died, Romance
died from English politics."[27] He served in Parliament from 1889 until
his death; he was Chief Secretary for Ireland from 1900 to 1905 and
put through the Irish Land Act of 1903. It was during the time after
1892, when his party was out of power, that he met William Ernest
Henley and interested himself in critical and scholarly enterprises. He
once wrote, with becoming modesty (a virtue that was never seen in
Steevens) that he was occupied in "riding these two circus horses,
Politics and Poetry, round the narrow arena of my capacity."[28]

He wrote an introduction to the Tudor Translations series edition of
North's Plutarch in 1895 and he brought out an edition of the *Poems* of
Shakespeare in 1898.

In his approach to the sonnets, Wyndham first made clear what he
considered lyric poetry to be: "We may say that the best lyrical and
elegiac poetry expresses, both by its meaning and its movement, the
quintessence of man's desire for Beauty, abstracted from concrete and
transitory embodiments. The matter of such poetry is 'Beauty that
must die'; the method, a succession of beautiful images flashed from a
river of pleasing sound."[29]

---

[26]*Ibid.*, pp. 12-13.
[27]*Men Were Different* (1937), p. 187.
[28]*Op. cit.*, p. 191.
[29]*The Poems of Shakespeare,* edited with an introduction by George Wyndham

Wyndham, unlike others who had been working on the sonnets at the time, did not attempt to identify the Fair Friend, the Dark Lady and the Rival Poet. Instead, he maintained, "The sonnets are, each one, in the first place lyrical and elegiac. They are concerned chiefly with the delight and pathos of Beauty, and they reflect this inspiration in their forms: all else in them, whether of personal experience or contemporary art, being mere raw material and conventional trick, exactly as important to these works of Shakespeare as the existence of the quarries at Carrara and the inspiration from antique marbles were to the works of Michelangelo."[30] To summarize, Wyndham held that Shakespeare "saw the beauty of this world both in the pageant of the year and the passion of his heart, and found for its expression the sweetest song that has ever triumphed and wailed over the glory of loveliness and the anguish of decay."[31]

Like later editors (e.g. Tucker Brooke and Brents Stirling) Wyndham saw the sonnets as falling into groups. In the first series, 1–125, he finds seven groups which almost constitute continuous poems, with occasional sonnets interspersed between two groups. His group F, containing Sonnets 87–96, is one in which "the theme of utter estrangement is handled with complete command over dramatic yet sweetly modulated discourse."[32] In his note on 94 ("They that have power to hurt and will do none") he maintains that it is "a limb of the continuous argument embodied in Group F . . . and, so read, is not obscure."[33]

Wyndham focuses his attention on the imagery, as any Keatsian admirer of the sonnets would do. The images, he says, are "often so vividly seized and so minutely presented as to engross attention, to the prejudice of the theme. Indeed, at some times the poet himself seems rather the quarry than the pursuer of his own images—as if it were a magician hounded by spirits of his own summoning."[34] Wyndham lists the various sources from which images are drawn: nature first of all, then inheritance, usury, law, navigation, husbandry, painting,

---

(1898), p. vii. The introduction was reprinted in *Essays in Romantic Literature* by George Wyndham, edited, with an introduction, by Charles Whibley, 1919.

[30]*Ibid.*, p. xiii.
[31]*Ibid.*, p. xviii.
[32]*Ibid.*, p. cxxii.
[33]*Ibid.*, p. 307
[34]*Ibid.*, p. cxxxii.

music, and "the Dark Sciences" (alchemy, astrology). He does not catalog them or draw inferences from them, as Caroline Spurgeon was later to do, but notes that some critics emphasize the vividness of the imagery and others "the magic of sound and association which springs from his unexpected collocation of words till then unmated."[35] When the imagery comes from nature, Wyndham holds, the first excellence is predominant; when it comes from the occupations of men, the second.

Wyndham does not overlook the technical aspects of versification. He points out the richness of alliteration and assonance in the poems. He is particularly sensitive to the distinctive qualities of rhyme and accent: "Shakespeare, in the Sonnets, whilst reveling in the joy of the rhyme, handed down from the French origin of English verse and confirmed by the imitation of Italian models, also turned the other and indigenous feature of English verse to the best conceivable advantage. No other English poet lets the accent fall so justly in accord with the melody of his rhythm and the emphasis of his speech, or meets it with a greater variety of subtly affiliated sounds."[36]

Wyndham's interest in sound texture and its relation to meaning is best illustrated in his comment on Sonnet I. He prints the sonnet in his introduction with significant sounds italicized:

> From *f*airest *cr*eatures we desi*re* in*cr*ease
> That thereby beauty's *R*ose might never *Die*
> But as the *R*iper should by *T*ime de*cease*
> His *t*ender he*ir* might be*ar* his memory.
> But thou con*tr*ac*ted* to thine own *bright eyes*
> Feed'st thy light's *f*lame with se*lf*-substantial *f*uel
> Making a *f*amine where *a*bundance *lies*,
> T*h*yself thy *f*oe to thy sweet self *too* c*ru*el
> T*h*ou that are n*ow* the world's fresh *o*rnament
> And *o*nly he*r*ald to the gaudy sp*ri*n*g*
> Withi*n* thine own *bud bur*iest thy con*tent*
> And *t*ender ch*url* mak'st w*a*s*te* in niggarding
> Pity the w*orl*d or else this *g*lutton *be*
> To *eat* the world's due by the *gr*ave and *thee.*

---

[35]*Ibid.*, p. cxxxiv.
[36]*Ibid.*, pp. cxli-cxlii.

Wyndham points out that the principal stresses in any one line are marked by alliteration or assonance or both. What he finds most characteristic of Shakespeare is "the juxtaposition of assonantal sounds where two syllables consecutive, but in separate words, are accented with a marked pause between them: —E.g., line 5 br*ight* *ey*es; line 8 *too cru*el. . . ." He is also aware of how these sound effects are important in the structure of the sonnet: "It is by this combination of Accent with Rhyme that Shakespeare links the lines of each quatrain in his Sonnets into one perfect measure. If you except two—'Let me not to the marriage of true minds' and 'The expense of spirit in a waste of shame'—you find that he does not, as Milton did afterwards, build up his sonnet, line upon line, into one monumental whole: he writes three lyrical quatrains, with a pronounced pause after the second and a couplet after the third."[37]

Anyone can make his own diagram of the sound effects in Sonnet 1, or indeed any of the sonnets; if he has a fine ear he may detect more examples, and more subtle ones, than Wyndham notices. The important thing is that Wyndham is reading the sonnets as poetry. It is a far cry from Steevens' readings, which sometimes leave the impression that for Steevens the sonnets were fourteen-line specimens of prose. What Steevens objected to on the grounds of botanical inaccuracy Wyndham cites as an example of "shere beauty of diction in Shakespeare's sonnets which has endeared them to poets".[38]

Such a poet was Edith Sitwell, who declared that Sonnet 19 "is one of the greatest sonnets in the English language, with its tremendous first lines":

> Devouring Time, blunt thou the lion's paws,
> And make the earth devour her own sweet brood;
> Pluck the keen teeth from the fierce tiger's [jaws],
> And burn the long-liv'd phoenix in her blood;

The huge, fiery, and majestic double vowels contained in "Devouring." and "lion's" . . . these make the line stretch onward and outward until it is overwhelmed, as it were, by the dust of death, by darkness, with the

---

[37]*Ibid.*, p. cxliii.
[38]"The canker-blooms have all as deep a dye / As the perfumëd tincture of the roses," (op. cit., p. cxlv).

muffling sounds, first of "blunt", then of the far thicker, more muffling sound of "paws" . . . The thick *p* of "paws" muffles us with night. The music is made more vast still by the fact that, in the third line, two long stretching double vowels are placed close together ("keen teeth") and that in the 4th there are two alliterative *b*'s—"burn" and "blood"—these give an added magesty, a gigantic balance.[39]

An ideal reader of the sonnets will of course be susceptible to imagery and also acutely aware of sound effects. But he may also be legitimately interested in the thought, the reflections, the philosophy (if that is not too ambitious a word) of these poems. For such a reader we may turn to a professional philosopher, George Santayana, though we should recall that Santayana began as a poet and that he, too, wrote sonnets. "We may observe in general", he wrote, "that Shakespeare's genius shines in the texture of his poems rather than in their structure, in imagery and happy strokes rather than in integrating ideas. His poetry plays about life like ivy about a house, and is more akin to land-scape than to architecture."[40]

Yet Santayana's most extensive comment is on Sonnet 146 ("Poor soul, the centre of my sinful earth"), the so-called "Christian sonnet":

This sonnet contains more than a natural religious emotion inspired by a single event. It contains reflection, and expresses a feeling not merely dramatically proper but rationally just. A mind that habitually ran into such thoughts would be philosophically pious; it would be spiritual. The Sonnets, as a whole, are spiritual; their passion is transmuted into discipline. Their love, which, whatever its nominal object, is hardly anything but love of beauty and youth in general, is made to triumph over time by a metaphysical transformation of the object into something eternal. At first this is the beauty of the race renewing itself by generation, then it is the description of beauty in the poet's verse, and finally it is the immortal soul enriched by the contemplation of that beauty. This noble theme is the more impressively rendered by being contrasted with another, with a vulgar love that by its nature refuses to be so transferred and transmuted. "Two loves," cries the poet, in a line that gives us the essence of the whole, "Two loves I have—of

---

[39]"A Note on Sonnet XIX" in *A Poet's Notebook* (1943), reprinted in *A Notebook on William Shakespeare* (1948), pp. 226-27.
[40]Introduction to Hamlet, Vol. 30 of *The Complete Works of Shakespeare*, with annotations and a general introduction by Sidney Lee (1908), p. xxiv.

comfort and despair." In all this depth of experience, however, there is still wanting any religious image. The Sonnets are spiritual, but with the doubtful exception of . . . [146] they are not Christian.[41]

Commenting further on Shakespeare's view of life in general, Santayana wrote to Logan Pearsall Smith about his book *On Reading Shakespeare*, on April 12, 1933,

And this brings me to your conclusion about his philosophy—that life is a dream. Yes, that is his philosophy: and when T. S. Eliot says that this philosophy (borrowed he thinks from Seneca) is an inferior one, compared with Dante's, I agree if you mean inferior morally and imaginatively: but it happens to be the true philosophy for the human passions, and for a man enduring, without supernaturally interpreting, the spectacle of the universe. It is a commonplace philosophy, the old heathen philosophy of mankind. Shakespeare didn't invent it. He felt it was true, and he never thought of transcending it.[42]

---

[41]"The Absence of Religion in Shakespeare," chap. 6 in *Interpretations of Poetry and Religion* (1900), pp. 151-52.

[42]*The Letters of George Santayana*, ed. Daniel Cory (1955), p. 250. The two treatments of Santayana as a critic of Shakespeare known to me are John M. Major, "Santayana on Shakespeare," *Shakespeare Quarterly* 10 (1959): 469-79; and Elkin Calhoun Wilson, *Shakespeare, Santayana and the Comic* (1973). Neither one deals with Santayana as a reader of the sonnets. I cannot pretend to thoroughness without quoting Santayana's translation of Shakespeare's Sonnet 29 ("When in disgrace with Fortune and men's eyes") into modern American:

When times are hard and old friends fall away
And all alone I lose my hope and pluck,
Doubting if God can hear me when I pray,
And brood upon myself and curse my luck,
Envying some stranger for his handsome face,
His wit, his wealth, his chances, or his friends,
Desiring this man's brains and that man's place,
And vexed with all I have that makes amends,
Yet in these thoughts myself almost despising,—
By chance I think of you; and then my mind,
Like music from deep sullen murmurs rising
To peals and raptures, leaves the earth behind;
    For if you care for me, what need I care
    To own the world or be a millionaire?

It was first published in *The New Republic* 2 (February 27, 1915): 17; it is reprinted in *The Genteel Tradition: Nine Essays by George Santayana*, ed. Douglas L. Wilson (1957), pp. 65-71.

It is apparent from this sample of readers of the sonnets that every reader is conditioned by his own time and by his own artistic-intellectual milieu. Steevens and Wyndham had the same texts before them, but they brought very different equipment to the experience of reading the poems. A reader of this book will bring to the reading of the sonnets still different equipment. It is not possible for an editor or critic to provide a reader in the penultimate decade of the twentieth century with the experience of a reader from the first decade of the seventeenth.[43] Even if it were possible, it is not at all clear that it would be desirable. What is valuable in the sonnets is what has endured beyond the concerns of 1609. Shakespeare often comments on this survival. In Sonnet 74 he tells the Fair Friend:

> My life hath in this line some interest,
> Which for memorial still with thee shall stay.
> When thou reviewest this, thou dost review
> The very part was consecrate to thee.
> ....
> The worth of that is that which it contains,
> And that is this, and this with thee remains.

An editor can and should explain the meaning of obsolete words or words that have changed their meaning. Both Booth and Empson have demonstrated that it is not difficult to *over*-explain, but they cannot put us in the frame of mind of a 1609 reader. The reader Booth tries to evoke is a post-Empson reader, and there was no such thing in 1609.

A twentieth-century reader who is at home in Elizabethan English and has an ear attuned to Elizabethan poetry will find many moving meditations in these sonnets. He will of course find much about Time and its ravages, particularly of its destruction of natural beauty but also of its demolition of monuments erected by man. He will often reflect on what age does to physical beauty:

> the glowing of such fire
> That on the ashes of his youth doth lie,
> As the death-bed whereon it must expire,
> Consum'd by that which it was nourish'd by.

(73.9–12)

---

[43]Stephen Booth says his edition "is explicitly designed to insure that a reader's experience of the sonnets will as far as possible approximate that of the first readers of the 1609 Quarto." *Shakespeare's Sonnets*, p. xii.

He will be reminded of death itself, not a figure of speech:

> The earth can yield me but a common grave,
> When you entombèd in men's eyes shall lie;
> Your monument shall be my gentle verse,
> Which eyes not yet created shall o'er-read,
> And tongues to be your being shall rehearse,
> When all the breathers of this world are dead.
>
> (81.7–12)

A reader of Shakespeare, whether of the plays or the poems, is often confronted with the contrast between the reality that is in the mind and the reality that is external to it:

> If the dull substance of my flesh were thought,
> Injurious distance should not stop my way,
> For then despite of space I would be brought
> From limits far remote, where thou dost stay.
>
> (44.1–4)

Even for a Shakespeare there is the experience of finding that one's words are inadequate to express one's feelings:

> Hearing you prais'd, I say, "'Tis so, 'tis true,"
> And to the most of praise add something more,
> But that is in my thought, whose love to you
> (Though words come hindmost) holds his rank before.
>
> (85.9–12)

As Santayana says, the sonnets are religious, but, with the possible exception of 146, are not Christian. Yet they show an understanding of worship:

> but yet like prayers divine,
> I must each day say o'er the very same,
> Counting no old thing old, thou mine, I thine,
> Even as when first I hallowed thy fair name.
>
> (108.5–8)

They distinguish true worship from idolatry in 105 ("Let not my love be call'd idolatry") and from fashionable superstition or pseudo-science:

> Not from the stars do I my judgment pluck,
> And yet methinks I have astronomy,
> But not to tell of good or evil luck,
> Of plagues, of dearths, or seasons' quality.
>
> (14.1–4)

In fact, the poet smiles at the failures of some prognosticators: ". . . sad augurs mock their own presage" (107.6).

Though he does not predict, as the almanacs do, the "seasons' quality," he is the ultimate poet of the seasons:

> Shall I compare thee to a summer's day?
>
> (18.1)

> How like a winter hath my absence been
> From thee, the pleasure of the fleeting year!
> What freezings have I felt, what dark days seen!
> What old December's bareness everywhere!
>
> (97.1–4)

> From you have I been absent in the spring,
> When proud-pied April, (dress'd in all his trim)
>
> (98.1–2)

> That time of year thou mayst in me behold
> When yellow leaves, or none, or few, do hang
> Upon those boughs which shake against the cold,
> Bare [ruin'd] choirs, where late the sweet birds sang.
>
> (73.1–4)

It must be granted that the acme of Shakespeare's seasons poetry is not in the sonnets, but in the two songs at the end of *Love's Labor's Lost*. They are in the form of a contest or *debat* between Spring and Winter, composed, according to the bombastic Armado, by "two learned men in praise of the owl and the cuckoo." Each song consists of two nine-line stanzas, which is larger than the sonnet's narrow room. The pastoral, lively atmosphere of spring, with its invigorating sexuality and its ironically fearful song of the cuckoo, contrasts strongly with the homely Breughelesque detail of the domestic winter scene, presided over by the staring owl.

The seasons in the sonnets are intertwined with concepts of love, but even then a bird is brought in:

> Our love was new, and then but in the spring,
> When I was wont to greet it with my lays,
> As Philomel in summer's front doth sing,
> And stops [her] pipe in growth of riper days:
> Not that the summer is less pleasant now
> Than when her mournful hymns did hush the night,

> But that wild music burthens every bough,
> And sweets grown common lose their dear delight.
>
> (102.5–12)

Celebration of love is naturally the central and most pervasive theme of the sonnets, and love, of course, has almost innumerable aspects. It is a major theme of Shakespeare's comedies and tragedies as well. The greatest sonnet on love is, I suppose, 116 ("Let me not to the marriage of true minds"), with its profound thought, rich imagery, its sonorous sound and its powerful declarative mode. The first quatrain of 124, for contrast, is less eloquent but more concise and knotty:

> If my dear love were but the child of state,
> It might for Fortune's bastard be unfather'd,
> As subject to time's love, or to Time's hate,
> Weeds among weeds, or flowers with flowers gather'd.

Here politics, Fortune, Time, and flowers are all brought together as possible threats to the speaker's "dear love." One might say of love in the sonnets that nothing in life is alien to it.

SELECTED BIBLIOGRAPHY

The following lists contain a very small part of the published material on Shakespeare's sonnets. I have included only items that seem to me helpful to readers of the sonnets as poetry. It should not be assumed that the omission of any contribution means that I have not read it; the inclusion of any item does not necessarily mean that I agree with its method or conclusions.

Annotated Editions

Alden, Raymond Macdonald, ed., *The Sonnets of Shakespeare*. Boston: Houghton Mifflin, 1916.

Booth, Stephen, ed., *Shakespeare's Sonnets*. New Haven: Yale University Press, 1977, 1978.

Brooke, Tucker, ed., *Shakespeare's Sonnets*. New York: Oxford University Press, 1936.

Burto, William, ed., *The Signet Classic Shakespeare: The Sonnets,* with an introduction by W. H. Auden. New York: New American Library, 1964.

Ingram, W. G. and Redpath, Theodore, eds., *Shakespeare's Sonnets*. New York: Barnes and Noble, 1965.

Rollings, Hyder Edward, ed., *A New Variorum Edition of Shakespeare: The Sonnets*. 2 vols. Philadelphia: Lippincott, 1944.

Tucker, T. G., ed., *The Sonnets of Shakespeare*. Cambridge: Cambridge University Press, 1924.

Wilson, John Dover, ed., *The New Shakespeare: The Sonnets*. Cambridge: Cambridge University Press, 1966.

Wyndham, George, ed., *The Poems of Shakespeare*. London: Methuen, 1898.

Collections of Criticism

Herrnstein, Barbara, ed., *Discussions of Shakespeare's Sonnets*. Boston: Heath, 1964.

Hubler, Edward, ed., *The Riddle of Shakespeare's Sonnets*. New York: Basic Books, 1962.

Jones, Peter, ed., *Shakespeare: The Sonnets: A Casebook*. London: Macmillan, 1977.

Landry, Hilton, ed., *New Essays on Shakespeare's Sonnets.* New York: AMS Press, 1976.

Nicoll, Allardyce, ed., *Shakespeare Survey 15.* Cambridge: Cambridge University Press, 1962.

Scholarly and Critical Works

Bernard, John D., " 'To Constancie Confinde': The Poetics of Shakespeare's Sonnets." *PMLA* 94 (1979):77–90.

Booth, Stephen, *An Essay on Shakespeare's Sonnets.* New Haven: Yale University Press, 1969.

Burckhardt, Sigurd, "The Poet as Fool and Priest": chap. 2 in *Shakespearean Meanings.* Princeton: Princeton University Press, 1968.

Colie, Rosalie, "Criticism and the Analysis of Craft": chap. 1 in *Shakespeare's Living Art.* Princeton: Princeton University Press, 1974.

Crutwell, Patrick, "Shakespeare's Sonnets and the 1590's": chap. 1 in *The Shakespearean Moment and its place in the Poetry of the Seventeenth Century.* London: Chatto & Windus, 1954. New York: Vintage Books, 1960.

Edwards, Philip, "The Sonnets to the Dark Woman": chap. 2 in *Shakespeare and the Confines of Art.* London: Methuen, 1968.

Ewbank, Inga-Stina, "Shakespeare's Poetry": chap. 7 in *A New Companion to Shakespeare Studies,* ed. S. Schoenbaum and Kenneth Muir. Cambridge: Cambridge University Press, 1971.

Ferry, Anne, "Shakespeare": chap. 1 in *All in War with Time.* Cambridge: Harvard University Press, 1975.

Gérard, Albert S., "The Stone as Lily." *Shakespeare Jahrbuch* 96 (1960): 155–60.

Goldsmith, Ulrich K., "Words Out of a Hat? Alliteration and Assonance in Shakespeare's Sonnets." *JEGP* 49 (1950):33–48.

Grivelet, Michel, "Shakespeare's 'War with Time': the Sonnets and 'Richard II'." *Shakespeare Survey* 23 (1970):69–78.

Hoy, Cyrus, "Shakespeare and the Revenge of Art." *Rice University Studies* 60 (1974):71–94.

Hubler, Edward, *The Sense of Shakespeare's Sonnets.* Princeton: Princeton University Press, 1952.

Jackson, MacD. P., "Punctuation and the Compositors of Shakespeare's Sonnets 1609." *Library* 5th series 30 (1975):1–24.

Kaula, David, " 'In War with Time': Temporal Perspectives in Shakespeare's Sonnets." *SEL* 3 (1963):45–57.

Knight, G. Wilson, *The Mutual Flame.* London: Methuen, 1955.

Knights, L. C., "Time's Subjects: The Sonnets and *King Henry IV, Part II*:" chap. 3 in *Some Shakespearean Themes.* London: Chatto and Windus, 1959.

Krieger, Murray, *A Window to Criticism: Shakespeare's Sonnets and Modern Poetics.* Princeton: Princeton University Press, 1964.

———, "Poetic Presence and Illusion." *Critical Inquiry* 5 (1979):616–17.

Landry, Hilton, *Interpretations in Shakespeare's Sonnets.* Berkeley and Los Angeles: University of California Press, 1963.

Leishman, J. B., *Themes and Variations in Shakespeare's Sonnets.* London: Hutchinson, 1961, 1963.

Lever, J. W., "Shakespeare": chap. 7 in *The Elizabethan Love Sonnet.* London: Methuen, 1956.

Levin, Richard, "Sonnet CXXIX as a 'Dramatic' Poem." *SQ* 16 (1965): 175–81.

Mahood, M. M., *Shakespeare's Wordplay.* London: Methuen, 1965.

Melchiori, Giorgio, *Shakespeare's Dramatic Meditations: An Experiment in Criticism.* London: Oxford University Press, 1976.

McCanless, Michael, "Increasing Store with Loss: Some Themes of Shakespeare's Sonnets." *TSLL* 13 (1971):391–406.

Neely, Carol Thomas, "Detachment and Engagement in Shakespeare's Sonnets: 94, 116, and 129." *PMLA* 92 (1977):83–95.

———, "The Structure of English Renaissance Sonnet Sequences." *ELH* 45 (1978):359–89.

Parker, David, "Verbal Moods in Shakespeare's Sonnets." *MLQ* 30 (1969): 331–39.

Piper, William Bowman, *Evaluating Shakespeare's Sonnets. Rice University Studies* 65 (1979):1–85.

Richmond, Hugh M., "The Sonnets: Reversal of Expectations in Love": chap. 2 in *Shakespeare's Sexual Comedy: A Mirror for Lovers.* Indianapolis: Bobbs-Merrill, 1971.

Roessner, Jane, "Double Exposure: Shakespeare's Sonnets 106–114." *ELH* 46 (1979):357–78.

Schaar, Claes, *An Elizabethan Sonnet Problem: Shakespeare's Sonnets, Daniel's Delia, and their Literary Background.* Lund, Sweden: *Lund Studies in English* 28, 1960.

———, *Elizabethan Sonnet Themes and the Dating of Shakespeare's Sonnets.* Lund, Sweden: *Lund Studies in English* 32, 1962.

Smith, Hallett, "The Sonnets": chap. 3 in *Elizabethan Poetry.* Cambridge: Harvard University Press, 1952.

Stirling, Brents, *The Shakespeare Sonnet Order: Poems and Groups.* Berkeley and Los Angeles: University of California Press, 1968.

Stookey, Lorena and Merrill, Robert, "Shakespeare's Fearful Meditation: Sonnet 94." *MLQ* 39 (1978):27–37.

Toliver, Harold E., "Shakespeare and the Abyss of Time." *JEGP* 64 (1965): 234–54.

Waddington, Raymond B., "Shakespeare's Sonnet 15 and the Art of Memory" in *The Rhetoric of Renaissance Poetry,* ed. Thomas O. Sloan and Raymond B. Waddington, pp. 96–122. Berkeley and Los Angeles: University of California Press, 1974.

Warren, Roger, "Why Does It End Well? Helena, Bertram, and the Sonnets." *Shakespeare Survey* 22 (1969):79–92.

———, "*A Lover's Complaint, All's Well,* and the Sonnets." *N&Q* 215 (1970):130–32.

West, Michael, "The Internal Dialogue of Shakespeare's Sonnet 146." *SQ* 25 (1974):109–22.

INDEX OF NAMES AND TOPICS

INDEX TO REFERENCES TO SONNETS

(An asterisk indicates that the sonnet is quoted in full)

47. Betwixt mine eye and heart a league is took 52, 91*, 111, 139
49. Against that time (if ever that time come) 17, 111*
51. Thus can my love excuse the slow offense 147
52. So am I as the rich whose blessed key 140
53. What is your substance, whereof are you made 16, 65
54. O how much more doth beauty beauteous seem 98, 147
55. Not marble nor the gilded [monuments] 33
56. Sweet love, renew thy force, be it not said 70–71, 142
57. Being your slave, what should I do but tend 101–102*
58. That god forbid that made me first your slave 103*
59. If there be nothing new, but that which is 33, 34*, 116, 117
60. Like as the waves make towards the pibbled shore 33, 116
61. Is it thy will thy image should keep open 143
62. Sin of self-love possesseth all mine eye 143
63. Against my love shall be as I am now 147–48
64. When I have seen by Time's fell hand defaced 33, 113*, 116
65. Since brass, nor stone, nor earth, nor boundless sea 33*, 113, 116
66. Tir'd with all these, for restful death I cry 45*, 117
67. Ah, wherefore with infection should he live, 21, 96, 117
68. Thus is his cheek the map of days outworn 96, 98*, 117
69. Those parts of thee that the world's eye doth view 21–22, 97, 117
70. That thou art blam'd shall not be thy defect 21, 98, 117, 120
71. No longer mourn for me when I am dead 17
72. O, lest the world should task you to recite 17, 44
73. That time of year thou mayst in me behold 148, 158, 160
74. But be contented when that fell arrest 158
75. So are you to my thoughts as food to life 142
76. Why is my verse so barren of new pride 36, 79, 86*, 142
77. Thy glass will show thee how thy beauties [wear] 37
78. So oft have I invok'd thee for my Muse 38
79. Whilst I alone did call upon thy aid 16, 36
80. O how I faint when I of you do write 38*
81. Or I shall live your epitaph to make 40, 159
82. I grant thou wert not married to my Muse 39, 79
83. I never saw that you did painting need 16, 39
85. My tongue-tied Muse in manners holds her still 40, 159
86. Was it the proud full sail of his great verse 38–39*
87. Farewell, thou art too dear for my possessing 5–6*, 18, 110
88. When thou shalt be dispos'd to set me light 18
89. Say thou didst forsake me for some fault 18
90. Then hate me when thou wilt, if ever, now 6–7, 18, 44–45
91. Some glory in their birth, some in their skill 25*
93. So shall I live, supposing thou art true 21, 117, 148
94. They that have pow'r to hurt, and will do none 2*, 18, 22, 106, 117, 153
95. How sweet and lovely dost thou make the shame 22
96. Some say thy fault is youth, some wantonness 22, 142
97. How like a winter hath my absence been 31–32*, 73*, 89, 160
98. From you have I been absent in the spring 74*, 89, 96, 160
102. My love is strength'ned, though more weak in seeming 89, 160–61